BUILD AN HTML5 GAME

BUILD AN HTML5 GAME

A Developer's Guide with CSS and JavaScript

by Karl Bunyan

no starch press

San Francisco

BUILD AN HTML5 GAME. Copyright © 2015 by Karl Bunyan.

Printed in USA

First printing

19 18 17 16 15   1 2 3 4 5 6 7 8 9

ISBN-10: 1-59327-575-7
ISBN-13: 978-1-59327-575-4

Text stock is SFI certified

Publisher: William Pollock
Production Editor: Alison Law
Cover Illustration: Garry Booth
Interior Design: Octopod Studios
Developmental Editor: Jennifer Griffith-Delgado
Technical Reviewer: Patrick H. Lauke
Copyeditor: Anne Marie Walker
Compositor: Susan Glinert Stevens
Proofreader: James Fraleigh

For information on distribution, translations, or bulk sales, please contact No Starch Press, Inc. directly:

No Starch Press, Inc.
245 8th Street, San Francisco, CA 94103
phone: 415.863.9900; info@nostarch.com
www.nostarch.com

Library of Congress Cataloging-in-Publication Data:

Bunyan, Karl.
  Build an HTML5 game : a developer's guide with CSS and JavaScript / by Karl Bunyan.
      pages cm
  Includes index.
  Summary: "A hands-on guide to web game development for programmers interested in building games for web and mobile using HTML5, CSS, and JavaScript"-- Provided by publisher.
   ISBN 978-1-59327-575-4 -- ISBN 1-59327-575-7
  1. Computer games--Programming. 2. Web applications. 3. HTML (Document markup language) 4. JavaScript (Computer program language) 5. Cascading style sheets. I. Title.
   QA76.76.C672B856 2015
   794.8'1526--dc23

                                        2014040059

About the Author

Karl Bunyan began his programming career in the early 1980s, writing adventure games on the Sinclair ZX Spectrum. His first game was published in 1990, and he took his first steps in Internet development in 1998. After three years of developing websites, touchscreen displays, interactive television applications, and CD-ROM projects for web agencies, Karl started his own consultancy business.

Since 2008, Karl has developed a number of games for the Facebook platform, ranging from traditional turn-based puzzlers to complex resource-management games, including HTML5 prototypes for the Game Show Network. He has spoken at events such as the Facebook Developer Garage in London and the HTML5 Developer's Conference, and he is the owner of Wedu Games, an independent firm that builds web and mobile games.

About the Technical Reviewer

Patrick H. Lauke works as an accessibility consultant for The Paciello Group. In a previous life he was a web evangelist in the developer relations team at Opera Software ASA, and before that he worked as a web editor for a large UK university for nearly 10 years. He's been involved in the discourse around web standards and accessibility since 2001, speaking at conferences and actively participating in initiatives such as the Web Standards Project (WaSP). An outspoken accessibility and standards advocate, Patrick favors a pragmatic hands-on approach over purely theoretical, high-level discussions. His personal corner of the Web can be found at *http://www.splintered.co.uk/*.

BRIEF CONTENTS

CONTENTS IN DETAIL

PART 1
BUILDING A GAME WITH HTML, CSS, AND JAVASCRIPT

1
PREPARATION AND SETUP   3

2
SPRITE ANIMATION USING JQUERY AND CSS   29

3
GAME LOGIC
43

4
TRANSLATING GAME STATE CHANGES TO THE DISPLAY
69

PART 2
ENHANCEMENTS WITH HTML5 AND THE CANVAS

5
CSS TRANSITIONS AND TRANSFORMATIONS
93

PREFACE

Even among experienced web developers, I often hear the question, "What exactly is HTML5?" The answer is difficult, in part because the rate of technological advances means the answer may change from one week to the next. The term *HTML5* also tends to be used to bundle a collection of techniques, and those techniques are often judged by their end effect rather than the technology that created them.

Because of the uncertainty surrounding the term HTML5, the label of *HTML5 game programmer* has acquired a mystique, as if moving from web developer to game programmer requires superpowers. Thus the reason for this book: to demystify the transition from building web pages to building web games.

The challenge of writing a book on web technology is that the digital world moves so much faster than the physical one. Fashions and practices change while a book moves from first draft to publication, and technologies advance at such a pace that a book risks being obsolete from the day it's published. Thankfully, the path for HTML5 has been laid down by the World Wide Web Consortium (W3C) with the support of the major browser vendors, so my challenge was less about guessing which HTML5 features to include and more about considering when these features might be readily available for mainstream use. I was keen to write a practical how-to guide in the form of a tutorial, with techniques that could be used in the wild from day one, and I'm glad that features that were cutting edge when I wrote the initial draft are now supported by most web browsers.

Acknowledgments

Along the way, the input from the No Starch Press team has been invaluable in shaping the contents of this book. Thanks go to Keith Fancher, who initially made contact and suggested I start writing in the first place; Tyler Ortman, who set me on the right path after a very unstructured first draft; Alison Law, who kept the whole process moving along; and especially my editor, Jennifer Griffith-Delgado, without whom this book would have been twice as long and made half as much sense. I'd also like to thank my technical reviewer, Patrick Lauke, who was particularly invaluable in identifying areas where technology changed during the time between initial draft and final version.

I'm also grateful to a host of former co-workers and bosses who put up with—and often even encouraged—my playing with fun effects when I should have been working on paid projects. And finally, I'd like to thank my partner, Ann, whose goading about how long it was taking me to finish the book ensured that I didn't give up entirely.

INTRODUCTION

 Games are everywhere, and they're increasingly played on connected web devices and within desktop and mobile browser environments. As browser-based games become more popular, players are turning to sites like Facebook to discover simple, casual games that don't require a disc or much up-front setup to play. A game is just another link to click through.

During the past decade, improvements to Adobe's Flash plug-in contributed to the growth of the web browser as a gaming platform. Most browsers supported Flash, giving game developers access to a powerful platform that approached the dream of *write once, run anywhere*. HTML-based games have been around about as long, and you may even have played some (possibly without noticing). However, until recently, the use of HTML and JavaScript as a gaming platform played second fiddle to Flash due to graphics, sound, and speed limitations. But browsers and mobile gaming platforms have vastly improved, and the status quo is changing. Mobile operating systems have steered away from Flash as a supported plug-in, and as a result, game developers need tools that provide similar performance and flexibility while retaining the ubiquity that Flash had.

Browsers have also seen a rapid improvement in graphical and sound capabilities over the past few years. The rise in power of HTML mirrors increasing demand for a platform that delivers rich gaming experiences and has the backing of multiple platform providers. A well-supported, open platform is considered less likely to fall foul of commercial controls and a walled-garden mentality, and HTML5 is such a platform.

However, in my experience, many game developers come to HTML5 looking to build the same type of games they would have built in Flash. HTML5 is certainly one of the best options: it has a huge user base (anyone with a modern web browser), and HTML5 and Flash have many similar capabilities and constraints. Despite this similarity, thinking of HTML5 as a Flash replacement is likely to lead to disappointing product launches and missed opportunities. This is because the strengths of one do not directly map to the strengths of the other. Also, HTML5 is still in a relatively early stage of development. The platform is advancing rapidly, and it can be difficult to keep up with which new features are supported from month to month.

Much as with building a good web application, the key to making a successful game is to understand your platform's capabilities and restrictions. You have to design and build games that maximize the platform's potential while avoiding or minimizing its limitations. This book is intended as a first step in understanding what you can achieve with JavaScript, HTML, and CSS and introducing the methods by which you can do so.

Why Build HTML5 Games?

Before I dive into specifics about this book, let's step back and consider why you might want to create a game on the HTML5 platform in the first place.

Using Skills You Already Have

Web developers who are skilled with JavaScript and CSS will feel more confident about stepping into HTML5 game development. Deploying HTML and JavaScript files is also a familiar process, and you can build online components using server-side languages that overlap with web development.

But if you throw yourself into writing C++ or Objective-C, the combination of a new language, a new development environment, and new thought processes required for game development can be a steep learning curve. In short, the conceptual leap needed to move from web development to HTML5 game development is relatively minor compared to that needed for other game technologies.

Multi-environment Development

Many platforms have promised the ability to write once and run anywhere, and in my opinion, HTML5 is the closest that any technology has come to delivering. Whether you develop for a desktop browser or a packaged mobile application, your coding styles won't vary much, nor will the basic technology of representing objects on the screen and having a user interact with them. Of course, there will always be some environment-specific differences, especially if code is to take advantage of the features and benefits that one environment may have to offer over another.

Still, games written in HTML5 and JavaScript have a very good chance of working with minimal changes across multiple operating systems. This allows for simultaneous releases and single development teams rather than a team per system. You can also code and test in a desktop browser, even if the final environment will be different.

A Rapidly Improving Platform

HTML5 is constantly and rapidly improving. JavaScript's processing speed is also increasing, and sophisticated interpreters are approaching native speeds for some operations. Given the increases in CPU speed in the past 10 years, games written in JavaScript can perform better than many of those written in native code just a few years ago.

With the efforts of browser vendors and hardware manufacturers, this improvement trajectory will only continue, and there's no doubt that HTML5 is growing as a viable gaming platform. Whether HTML5 game development will grow as a fast development environment for immersive 3D games on mobile or desktop browsers or as a rapid prototyping environment for casual game developers, or even migrate into the console environment through Android or other devices, it's an exciting time to be a JavaScript programmer. Now is the time to build on the knowledge you will gain in this book and experiment with the capabilities of HTML5 and JavaScript as an open game development platform.

About This Book

This book cannot demonstrate the full range of possible HTML5 games and therefore does not explore the capabilities of HTML5 and JavaScript to the fullest. Instead, I concentrate on creating a single casual game, like those many developers have produced for years with Adobe Flash. These games are generally two-dimensional and single player with relatively short game loops. Advances in 3D capabilities, such as WebGL, mean that large, complex, immersive multiplayer games are either possible now or just around the corner, but a casual game project is a more natural place for a game developer to start. Simple projects also make it easier to illustrate the fundamental principles involved in building a game.

Who This Book Is For

This book is intended for web developers familiar with HTML, CSS, and JavaScript who want to translate their existing skills to game development. At the bare minimum, you should know how to program, and ideally, you should know the basics of JavaScript. You should also have access to a web server and development environment of your own or be able to set those up for yourself.

If you have some background knowledge in either web or gaming technologies, want to know what you could achieve with HTML5, and have the enthusiasm to learn and experiment, you should be able to work through this book. By the end, you'll have a clear idea of how to approach HTML5 game development projects and a good overview of the core processes involved in making games in general.

Overview

Throughout the book, you will develop a simple bubble-popping game meant to be played in a browser. With each chapter, I'll introduce new concepts by putting them into practice.

In **Part 1: Building a Game with HTML, CSS, and JavaScript**, which includes the first four chapters of the book, you'll build a complete game using HTML, CSS, and JavaScript.

- **Chapter 1: Preparation and Setup** looks at the tools we'll need, including the jQuery and Modernizr script libraries, how to debug, and how to put the game's file structure in place.

- **Chapter 2: Sprite Animation Using jQuery and CSS** describes how to move HTML elements around the screen in response to mouse clicks. In the context of the game, this means shooting an image from a starting position to the coordinates that the player clicks.

- **Chapter 3: Game Logic** has you draw the game board and set up much of the game logic, including firing a bubble and collision detection.

- **Chapter 4: Translating Game State Changes to the Display** teaches you to make the game respond to the collisions that we detected in Chapter 3 and add more game logic to pop groups of bubbles. This introduces some basic animation within an object by way of a popping effect.

In **Part 2: Enhancements with HTML5 and the Canvas**, you'll improve the game you created in Part 1 with features from HTML5 and the canvas.

- **Chapter 5: CSS Transitions and Transformations** shows you how to use CSS3 to achieve some of the results that you used jQuery for in previous chapters.

- **Chapter 6: Rendering Canvas Sprites** shows you how to render the game entirely within the HTML5 canvas, including moving objects across the screen and animation effects.

- **Chapter 7: Levels, Sound, and More** tidies up some loose ends in the game logic, introduces smoother animation techniques, and shows you how to implement sound effects and save the player's score.

- **Chapter 8: Next Steps in HTML5** discusses some useful technologies that you didn't need to use in the casual game you developed. It suggests areas for future reading, such as Web Workers and WebGL for 3D games, and discusses important issues, such as memory management and optimizing for speed.

- Finally, the **Afterword** provides some ideas to improve your HTML5 game-programming skills. For example, you could continue to improve on the game you built in this book, or you could start developing game ideas of your own.

All the code created in this book is available to download from *http://buildanhtml5game.com/*, where you can also see a version of the game you'll be building in action. And at the end of each chapter, I include exercises to test your skills and spark ideas for improving the *Bubble Shooter* game.

Depth of Coverage

Because this book focuses on casual game development, I won't go into detail about WebGL, three-dimensional modeling, shaders, textures, lighting, and other techniques associated with more complex games like first-person action shooters or massively multiplayer online role-playing games (MMORPGs). These subjects fill books all on their own. However, you'll find most principles of building casual games useful in more technically demanding situations. I recommend keeping your initial projects achievable and working toward something more complex after you have a few releases under your belt. Once you've completed a couple of projects using HTML, CSS, and the canvas, you'll be equipped to learn more about WebGL if that's a direction you want to pursue; however, you may find that you have more than enough development opportunities in the casual game space.

This book introduces you to game development techniques, but it is not an exhaustive reference for the Application Programming Interfaces (APIs) you'll use. Neither is it a complete guide to HTML5: only the features that are most relevant to game development are covered. The Internet is full of material that not only provides more detail but is also updated to reflect the ever-changing browser environment. I'll highlight useful resources and documentation as appropriate.

Likewise, this is not a book about game design. I'll teach you *how* to build, but not *what* to build. The skills you learn should give you a starting point from which you can bring your own ideas to life or start to work on projects designed by others.

How to Use This Book

Throughout the book, I'll help you create the HTML, CSS, and JavaScript files that form the *Bubble Shooter* game. You should keep the file *index.html* (created in Chapter 1) open in at least one browser at all times as you work through the tutorial. That way, you can refresh the page to see how your changes to the code have altered the game.

I encourage you to run the *Bubble Shooter* on a local development web server rather than viewing it from the filesystem so you can access it as a real user would and see how it looks on mobile devices.

NOTE *If you don't want to type the example code, just download the source code (from http://buildanhtml5game.com/) and work from the game files for the chapter you're reading.*

Once you've decided how you want to load the *Bubble Shooter* files for testing, jump into Chapter 1 to start making your first game!

PART 1

BUILDING A GAME WITH HTML, CSS, AND JAVASCRIPT

1

PREPARATION AND SETUP

In this chapter, we'll begin to develop a full game using HTML, CSS, and JavaScript. Our simple bubble shooter game will demonstrate a range of development techniques, but it won't need extensive logic to control the mechanics. *Game logic* includes systems for interaction between in-game elements, events that result from the player's actions, simulation of artificial intelligence in characters, and so on. Developing intricate game logic can be time-consuming, so for learning purposes, we'll stick with basic principles, such as how to render graphics and animation, respond to user input, and play sounds.

We'll start with the user interface and page layout, then load scripts, and finally add some basic interaction. During development, we'll also explore some browser tools that will prove helpful (especially when debugging), as well as Modernizr and jQuery—two main libraries that will speed up development. We'll use Modernizr to load scripts and detect whether a user's browser supports a given feature, and we'll use jQuery when working with HTML and JavaScript together.

If you're experienced in web application development using HTML, CSS, JavaScript, and jQuery, much of the code in this chapter will be familiar to you. My aim is to demonstrate what you can achieve with relatively little code and how easy it is to create basic interactive elements.

How the Game Is Played

If you've ever played *Puzzle Bobble*, *Bust-a-Move*, *Snood*, or any of the many mobile bubble-shooting games, you already know the basic mechanics of a bubble shooter. Figure 1-1 shows a screenshot of the finished game.

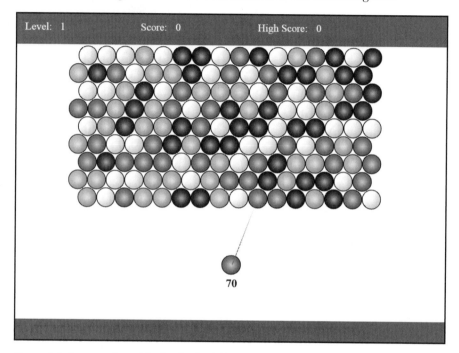

Figure 1-1: A screenshot of the finished Bubble Shooter *game*

The goal of the game is to clear all of the bubbles hanging from the top of the screen. The player aims with the mouse and clicks to fire a bubble from the bottom of the screen into the bubbles at the top, in hopes of forming groups of three or more bubbles of the same color. Once a matching color group of at least three bubbles is formed, all of the bubbles in the group burst, as shown in Figure 1-2.

If a bubble is fired and doesn't form a group that matches by color, it is added to the display, as shown in Figure 1-3.

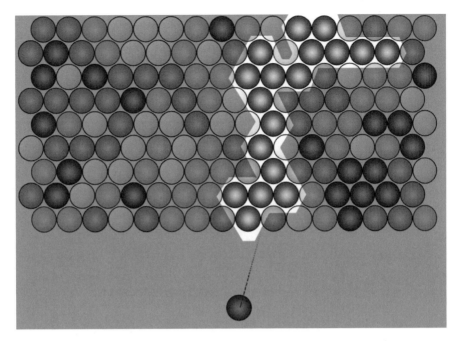

Figure 1-2: The blue bubble is fired at the group, creating a match, and all of the highlighted bubbles will pop.

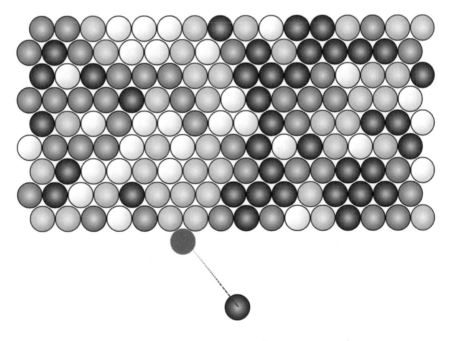

Figure 1-3: The blue bubble fired here won't cause the green group above it to pop. Instead, it will be added to the board.

Fired bubbles that don't form a matching group of three or more stick in the bubble grid. Because bubbles behave as if they're all hanging from the top row, if a set of bubbles can't trace a connection back to the top after a matching color group is created and removed, we need to remove those "orphaned" bubbles from the screen. An example of an orphaned bubble is shown Figure 1-4.

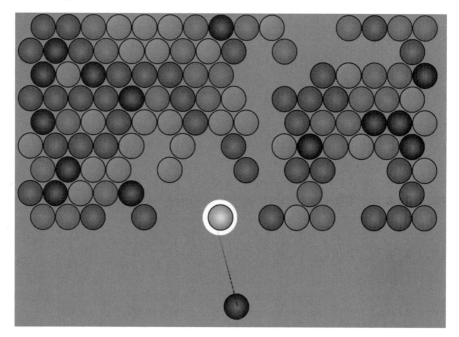

Figure 1-4: The red bubble is orphaned. We don't want to leave orphaned bubbles hanging, so we'll need some logic to detect them and an animation to remove them from the screen.

Players can fire only a limited number of bubbles (Figure 1-1 shows 70), and they must clear the board before they run out of bubbles to shoot. At the end of each level, the player scores points for popping bubbles and progresses to the next level. The game ends when the player fails to clear a level.

Short of a couple of enhancements that we'll add later, that's the main flow of the game.

We'll build the game mechanics using HTML, CSS, and JavaScript—core tools that are well suited to creating many simple games, especially two-dimensional games that don't require detailed pixel manipulation. In *Bubble Shooter*, we're essentially firing a circle (the bubble) into a grid of other circles (bubbles) and then either popping a group, as in Figure 1-2, or adding the bubble to the board, as in Figure 1-3. The demands of the game's layout are fairly simple, and we can use CSS and JavaScript to perform all of the animation we'll need.

We'll build the user interface in HTML and CSS because like most HTML games, *Bubble Shooter* will take advantage of the tasks the browser can do well, such as laying out text and rendering simple graphics. In later chapters, we'll explore using the canvas element to display the game area, but I'll first demonstrate what you can achieve with regular Document Object Model (DOM)–based development.

Building the Game

Now that we have an idea of the game we want to create, let's break it down into manageable tasks. We'll need to solve a number of high-level challenges to create *Bubble Shooter*. Specifically, we need to do the following:

Randomize and render the game board
> The bubble grid must be randomly generated and drawn onscreen for each new level.

Calculate the firing angle and stopping point for a bubble
> The player will fire bubbles by clicking on the screen. We'll calculate the angle at which to fire the bubble, move it along that path, and either stop it when it hits something or let it continue.

Resolve collisions
> When the fired bubble hits another bubble and does not form a matching group of three or more, it will add itself to the board. Otherwise, when it does form a group of at least three bubbles of the same color, it will pop all bubbles of that color contiguous with the one it strikes. If the fired bubble does pop bubbles, we'll check to see if we've created any orphaned bubbles, such as those shown in Figure 1-4.

Keep track of score and levels
> The game ends when all the bubbles are cleared. Because the player has only a limited number of bubbles to fire, we'll track the number of bubbles fired. We'll also add a scoring system to give the player a reason to play again (to beat a high score, for example).

Handle the game's end and new levels
> If a player completes a level, we'll indicate that (using certain interface elements) and give the player an option to progress to the next level. Changing levels clears the board and tidies up the internal game state, and then the game starts again.

Development and Testing Environment

Let's set up our development environment and make sure we have the right tools to complete the game. To start developing games for the Web, you'll need access to a range of browsers to test in and software that allows you to edit code. You'll also need to set up a web server to view the game in development. Although you can run *Bubble Shooter* locally (simply by opening its *index.html* file), you should regularly test your games in situations that match those of your end users as closely as possible.

NOTE *The process of setting up a server varies by operating system. The Apache web server (available at* http://httpd.apache.org/) *has good installation packages and instructions for setting up on most system configurations.*

Web Browser Testing

One rule of web development is to test on all browsers that you expect your target audience to use. Although this is essential for released software, while developing you can usually use a slightly smaller subset of browsers to identify most potential problems. The list of browsers you need to test on changes constantly, but when you release a game onto the Web, those discussed next are essential.

Desktop Browsers

Users of a desktop PC or laptop could end up playing your game in various browsers on any operating system, so be sure to test at least the latest versions of Internet Explorer (IE), Firefox, Chrome, and Safari for Windows and OS X. Depending on your target audience, you may need to test earlier browser versions as well.

Not everyone updates their web browsers, so when coding for a mass web audience, be sure not to ignore users who might be using earlier versions. Some versions of IE do not play well together on the same operating system (due to IE's tight integration with Windows), so when testing, you'll need multiple Windows installations available, either on different PCs or on virtual machines. I strongly suggest you install and use virtual machine software, such as VMWare (*http://www.vmware.com/*), VirtualBox (*http://www.virtualbox.org/*), or Virtual PC (*http://www.microsoft.com/download/*; search in the Download Center). Virtual machines allow you to run operating systems within your regular operating system, essentially simulating an entire system from your desktop. Virtual machines preinstalled with different versions of IE can be downloaded from *http://www.modern.ie/en-us/virtualization-tools/*.

Because Firefox now updates regularly, you should be able to safely test your games on the latest release. Earlier versions have patchy HTML5 support, but later versions rarely have major changes from one release to the next. Chrome updates automatically and regularly as well, so you don't need to worry about versions; just make sure you're running the latest one.

And, of course, you should also test your game on a Mac in at least one version of Safari. It's also possible to run an OS X virtual machine within Windows, although the setup is slightly more complex than running Windows within Windows or Windows within OS X. Tutorials are available online for achieving this setup within the virtual machine applications listed earlier.

Mobile Browsers

If you're deploying on mobile devices or tablets, testing on a wide range of devices (iOS, Android, and Windows mobile) and multiple browsers is more important than ever. For basic mobile development, access to one iOS device and one Android device may be sufficient for testing, but when you're considering wider distribution, the plot thickens. Apple's iOS versions vary in their behavior, and Android comes in so many flavors on so many devices with differing screen resolutions and hardware configurations that you should have access to multiple devices (perhaps through a limited beta testing group) for testing. We won't be packaging *Bubble Shooter* for release in the Apple App Store or Google Play Store, but by virtue of writing the game using HTML5 and JavaScript, we'll produce an app that's playable on mobile devices without extra coding.

Ultimately, due to the fragmentation of the Android platform, it's impossible for a single developer to test on every device; therefore, you may find it more viable to use a third-party testing service. Testing on iOS devices is slightly simpler because Apple controls its operating system and device specifications, but iPhones and iPads can be costly. When you add Windows tablets into the mix and consider the growing range of tablets and other portable devices that can run a web browser, you'll realize that the mobile testing battle is difficult to win.

Debugging in the Web Browser

With your test browsers set up, you can then use several developer tools to make debugging easy. Each browser has its own development tool set, but fortunately, they all operate along similar lines, provide ways to inspect HTML elements on the page, and add breakpoints and logging to JavaScript. Learn how to access your browser's developer tools and experiment with them to become familiar with their capabilities.

All browser debugging tools are useful, but you'll likely use the JavaScript console the most during development. You'll interact with your code through the console in two main ways:

Logging to the console with the `console.log` command
Call the `console.log` function, and the console should display the contents of whatever you pass into the function. For example, `console.log("Hello")` should display the string `Hello`. Even better, call `console.log` with a JavaScript object or array, and you'll get a limited listing of the object's contents that you can use to explore entire object trees.

Running ad hoc code to interrogate variable states
You can enter JavaScript code into the console to evaluate it immediately. Enter `alert(1)` into the console to see how it works. If your game code exposes object properties publicly, you can use this feature to examine properties or trigger methods. You can even paste in multiple lines of code to create and run entire functions in the context of the page.

Now that we have some of the tools we need, let's start building the game. We'll begin by setting up the basic code and implementing the start screen user interface.

Laying Out the Game Screen

Before we can program the fun parts of animation and gameplay, we need to lay out the user interface. We'll use HTML and CSS to place the main interface elements; the game screen will consist of three major areas, shown in Figure 1-5.

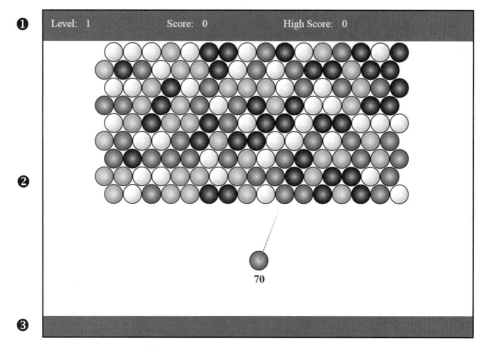

Figure 1-5: Sections of the game screen

At the top of the game screen, you can see the status bar ❶, which will show score and level information. The next (and largest) section contains the game area ❷, which will contain all the bubbles. The game area is also where the actual gameplay will happen. The footer ❸ at the bottom of the game screen frames the game area.

Now, let's lay out these three *Bubble Shooter* components.

Creating Panels with HTML and CSS

Using straightforward HTML and CSS to lay out the game screen is the easiest way to create the three panels and define where the action happens. The approach and techniques used here are identical to those used in building a regular website or web application.

We'll start by creating a wrapper div for the entire page. Because the div tag has no semantic meaning, we'll use it to denote a division on the page. Make a new folder in your web server's root directory to build the game in and call it *bubbleshoot*. Every file needed to run the game will be stored in this folder or within a subdirectory of it. Next, create a new file called *index.html* and add the following code:

index.html
```
<!DOCTYPE HTML>
<html lang="en-US">
  <head>
    <meta charset="utf8">
    <title>Bubble Shooter</title>
  </head>
  <body>
❶    <div id="page">
    </div>
  </body>
</html>
```

The entire game will run within this single HTML page, and the "page" div ❶ will constrain the area in which the game happens. If we ever need to center the game or move it to fit into unusual screen aspect ratios, we need only change the position of the wrapper element.

NOTE   *Many HTML tags have been simplified in version 5, in contrast to the relative strictness in versions 3 to 4 and XHTML. For example, the doctype declaration is now vastly simplified because many tags are assigned a default type. The <script> tag actually defaults to JavaScript in HTML5, which is why we don't need to specify type="text/javascript" or language="javascript" in our page.*

Next, we'll create three new div elements, one for each of the three page sections, and place them inside our page div:

```
<div id="page">
  <div id="top_bar"></div>
  <div id="game"></div>
  <div id="footer_bar"></div>
</div>
```

Now, we need to assign some CSS to our page and the three sections we just added.

Create a folder called _css in the game folder to contain all the style sheets we'll use for the game. In the _css folder, make a new file called *main.css* that contains the following code:

main.css

```
body
{
  margin: 0;
}
#page
{
  position: absolute;
  left: 0;
  top: 0;
  width: 1000px;
❶ height: 738px;
}
#top_bar
{
  position: absolute;
  left: 0;
  top: 0;
  width: 1000px;
❷ height: 70px;
  background-color: #369;
  color: #fff;
}
#game
{
  position: absolute;
  left: 0px;
  top: 70px;
  width: 1000px;
❸ height: 620px;
  background-color: #fff;
  clip: auto;
❹ overflow: hidden;
}
#footer_bar
{
  position: absolute;
  left: 0;
  top: 690px;
  width: 1000px;
❺ height: 48px;
  background-color: #369;
}
```

We'll make the top banner 70 pixels high ❷ and the bottom one 48 pixels high ❺. We want the game to fit in a standard monitor size, so we set the total game area to be 620 pixels high ❸, resulting in a total page height of 738 pixels ❶, which should fit within a 1024×768 display and even allow for a browser taskbar.

These values set the size and position of the entire usable display area. Also, notice that game has `overflow:` set to `hidden` ❹, which means that the bubbles in the game will never accidentally display over the header or footer.

To link up the CSS file, we'll add a file link for *main.css* to the HTML header:

index.html

```
<head>
  <meta charset="utf8">
  <title>Bubble Shooter</title>
  <link href="_css/main.css" rel="stylesheet">
</head>
```

Now that we've created the basic structure for *Bubble Shooter* with HTML and CSS, load the page in a browser and keep it open. There's no interaction yet, so next we'll add basic interactivity, such as a *start game* dialog, before we work on the game logic. The first step is to set up the coding structure.

Code Structure

Let's take a high-level look at the main concepts of the game and interface, which will guide how we'll structure the code. With a number of significant elements to implement, we'll structure the code in a way similar to the Model/View/Controller (MVC) principles that you may be familiar with from web application development. If MVC is new to you, here's the basic setup:

- The **Model** consists of data and maintains the state of the application. In a web application, this might be user's details or shopping cart contents, for example.

- The **View** renders what's on the screen and intercepts user input. For web applications, this is generally HTML output. For example, a view might read the contents of an online shopping cart from the *Model* and then display those items in a list.

- The **Controller** manages the logic and processing. For example, clicking an item in a *View* sends a message to the *Controller* to add a new item to a shopping cart *Model*.

With some alterations, this MVC principle will work for structuring *Bubble Shooter*.

Game Controller

The game controller will keep track of the game state and act as a director to determine outcomes in response to user actions.

The game controller is similar to a controller in the MVC system; it will run the game and manage all the functions. In a more complex game, a single controller would become too big and complicated to handle every task, because there would be too much code in one place and one set of code would have too many responsibilities, making the code more prone to bugs that would be harder to find. In that case, we'd probably need to subdivide the tasks further. Fortunately, because *Bubble Shooter* is so simple, using one controller to manage all tasks should work well.

User Interface Code

The game needs to display all kinds of information for the user, including score updates, level end screens, and so on. Instead of the game controller handling these tasks, it will instruct a set of user interface functions to control the way the user interface elements appear and disappear.

You could put much of the UI code into the game controller, but you'll often end up writing as much animation and UI code as game logic, so it's best to separate the code for readability. Generally, if you're not changing the state of the game in some way but instead are managing a function in the display, you should do that in the UI code.

Game Elements as Objects

We'll code a few game elements as objects, including the bubbles and the game board. The reason is that we'll have properties—x- and y-coordinates for the bubbles, for example—and methods to apply, such as bubbles popping. Following object-oriented programming convention, we'll split those objects into separate classes so the code structure maps to the conceptual elements involved in making the game.

The game's objects will also align closely with the idea of a model in the MVC web pattern. Objects will have properties and state, but they really shouldn't interact with the display or make significant gameplay decisions.

Adding the First Scripts

We'll use *Modernizr*, a JavaScript library, to load in all of the JavaScript files the game will need, such as the game controller and the UI class mentioned earlier. Using Modernizr has some advantages over using conventional <script> tags, and I'll explain those later in this chapter. Modernizr has other useful features as well, but we'll start by loading in the script files we need.

The Modernizr and jQuery Libraries

To short-cut some common tasks throughout the development of the game, we'll rely heavily on two libraries. Both libraries solve many cross-browser problems and provide high-level functions in a simple and consistent instruction set.

Modernizr will load scripts and detect whether a given feature is available in a browser. As an example, let's write some code to detect whether the canvas element is supported. To code this by hand, you would create a canvas node within the DOM and then check whether or not it supports a given method. In this example, we'll use the canvas element's getContext method, which is supported everywhere that canvas is supported, although you could try any canvas method you like:

```
var element = document.createElement("canvas");
var canvasSupported = !!element.getContext;
```

With Modernizr, we don't have to do as much work. We can simply write:

```
var canvasSupported = Modernizr.canvas;
```

The Modernizr object contains a set of properties whose values are set at load time to either true or false, depending on whether a particular feature is supported or not by the browser. As such, the variable canvasSupported should now contain either true or false, depending on the value of Modernizr.canvas. Using Modernizr to check for features is helpful because if a browser changes how it implements a feature, Modernizr will likely receive new detection routines faster than you can detect and implement the change within your codebase.

jQuery also provides useful shorthand functions, but these largely involve detecting and responding to events, making Asynchronous JavaScript and XML (AJAX) requests to communicate with a server or accessing and manipulating HTML elements in the browser's DOM.

The DOM is the browser's internal organization of an HTML document, and we'll primarily use jQuery's DOM access methods to simplify much of the animation code. The DOM provides a way for you to manipulate the structure of the HTML by exposing each element in the HTML as a DOM node. To manipulate the DOM, we first use JavaScript to select a node. We can then change one or more of its properties, which is possible and relatively straightforward with regular JavaScript. But using jQuery makes the code more likely to work as intended without writing code to handle browsers that implement individual features differently.

The most trivial example of jQuery in action is selecting a DOM node with an ID, such as the game div we've created. In conventional JavaScript, we would write this as

```
var element = document.getElementById("game");
```

This line of code retrieves a single DOM element, which will have various properties, such as its CSS formatting and methods that allow it to be interrogated. For example, `element.getAttribute("id")` will return the string game.

jQuery provides a way to wrap this functionality, and more, in a simpler, more compact syntax. To achieve the same result as the preceding code line with jQuery, we use jQuery selectors. *Selectors* are syntax for selecting a node or nodes within the DOM, and their format—including dot notation and using # to select unique elements—is borrowed from CSS selectors. The values returned from jQuery's selectors aren't DOM nodes but rather custom objects that contain a reference to the DOM nodes and add a range of other methods. The equivalent of `document.getElementById("game").getAttribute("id")` using a jQuery selector is `$("#game").attr("id")`.

Selectors are a core jQuery concept, and you'll become very familiar with using them by the end of this book. Nearly all of jQuery is used to manipulate DOM elements, so calls to jQuery almost always specify which element or elements should be changed, and that's where selectors come in. They let you choose an HTML node set using a range of factors, such as the following:

- A unique ID for selecting single elements
- A CSS class for selecting all the DOM elements with that class
- The tag that defines the node (`div`, `img`, `span`, and so on), which allows you, for example, to select all the images on a page
- Many other options, including combinations of the previous items in this list, the element's position in a list, parent-child relationships, or nearly any other way you can traverse a DOM

The jQuery object that the call to $ returns lets you manipulate the DOM object.

So in jQuery, the `document.getElementById` call is shortened to

```
var element = jQuery("#game").get(0);
```

We require the `.get(0)` function call to retrieve the DOM object from within the jQuery object, although generally it's more useful to work with jQuery objects than with DOM objects directly. This can be further shortened to

```
var element = $("#game").get(0);
```

The value $ is defined as an alias to the `jQuery` function, which does one of several tasks based on what you pass into it. For a selector, we pass a string value (in this case, `"#game"`) to jQuery. As in CSS, the hash symbol tells jQuery that we want to select a single element by its ID. The value `$("#game")` returns the jQuery object containing a reference to the DOM node.

You can use jQuery selectors to retrieve multiple DOM nodes, which are stored internally as an array. If you want to access the DOM node, you can retrieve the *n*th element returned from a query by calling .get(n) on the jQuery object. Because we have only one element with the ID game, we want the first (zero index) element, which we can retrieve by adding .get(0) onto the end of $("#game").

We don't save much coding in this simple case, but more important, we can use the objects that jQuery returns from selection queries with cross-browser methods that abstract away a lot of the hard work of DOM manipulation.

jQuery objects let us query the DOM node for various CSS properties, as in these examples:

```
var top = $("#game").css("top");
var width = $("#game").width();
var divs = $("div");
```

The first two lines query the DOM node for the game div's top position and width, respectively, and the last line is a selector that returns a jQuery object containing all the div tags on a page. jQuery is a powerful library, and although we'll use quite a few of its features in the game, covering it in great detail is beyond the scope of this book. The jQuery documentation at *http://api.jquery.com/* provides an in-depth look at how it works.

Adding the Modernizr Library

To get started with Modernizr, download it from its official website (*http://modernizr.com/download/*). Modernizr lets you choose individual features to download so you don't waste bandwidth on code that you'll never use. We'll need a few specific features, so make sure you select the following boxes on the download page to include them:

- CSS Transitions (under CSS3)
- Canvas and HTML5 Audio (under HTML5)
- Modernizr.load (under Extra)
- Modernizr.prefixed (under Extensibility)

Then, click **Generate** and **Download**.

Create a new folder in the game folder called *_js* and save the file there as *modernizr.js*. Also add the file to the HTML document, as shown here:

index.html
```
<head>
  <meta charset="utf8">
  <title>Bubble Shooter</title>
  <link href="_css/main.css" rel="stylesheet">
  <script src="_js/modernizr.js"></script>
</head>
```

Now that we've added Modernizr with a <script> tag, we'll use it to load the rest of the JavaScript game files.

Loading Scripts with Modernizr

Rather than just adding <script> tags to the document, we use Modernizr to load scripts for two main reasons. First, we can trigger functions to run immediately after a script is loaded rather than waiting until the entire page, including HTML and images, has loaded. Second, Modernizr allows us to load scripts in on a conditional basis (for example, *if this condition is satisfied, load in this script*) without writing much code to do it.

NOTE   *Modernizr actually uses another library called* yepnope.js *for its script-loading functionality. You can learn more about that library at* http://yepnopejs.com/.

A simple example of this is to load jQuery from Google's Content Delivery Network (CDN) to expedite load times. The potential flaw with using a third-party CDN is that the CDN could be down or inaccessible, or, more likely, your own server could be unavailable. However, relying on a service that you can't control is never a good idea. Fortunately, Modernizr lets you add a test during the loading process and then call a backup function if that test fails. As a result, we can attempt to load the file from the CDN, and if it doesn't work, load a local version instead.

WHY USE GOOGLE'S HOSTED JQUERY?

Although it may seem odd to rely on someone else's server to obtain a critical file, using Google's version of jQuery offers a few advantages, and I don't just mean saving money or using someone else's bandwidth should you create a popular game.

One advantage is that because the file comes from Google's Content Delivery Network, users will almost always download it from a server closer to them than your server.

Another advantage is that, because the file comes from a server other than the one your game is hosted on, users can actually download it faster. Browsers often limit the number of connections they'll open to a single server, so files wait in a queue to be downloaded, even if plenty of bandwidth is available. By hosting files on a different server, you increase the number of files that are downloaded in parallel and decrease the download time.

An additional advantage is that other sites are using the same copy of jQuery; therefore, if users have visited any of them recently, they'll most likely have a copy of the file in their browser cache and won't have to download the file at all!

Download the latest jQuery build from *http://jquery.com/download/* and place it in the *_js* folder. Then add the following code block in bold just before the closing </head> tag. Be sure to change the version of jQuery in the URLs to match the version that you've downloaded.

index.html

```
<head>
  <meta charset="utf8">
  <title>Bubble Shooter</title>
  <link href="_css/main.css" rel="stylesheet">
  <script src="_js/modernizr.js"></script>
  <script>
❶  Modernizr.load({
      load: "//ajax.googleapis.com/ajax/libs/jquery/1.8.2/jquery.js",
❷     complete: function () {
❸       if(!window.jQuery){
❹         Modernizr.load("_js/jquery-1.8.2.min.js");
        }
      }
    });
  </script>
</head>
```

This example shows the compact script loading Modernizr provides. In short, it attempts to load jQuery from the Google CDN ❶. When loading is finished ❷ (either when the file has loaded or the script returns from a failure to load), the `complete` property's function call checks for the existence of `window.jQuery` ❸, and if that object doesn't exist, loads the jQuery library from the local folder ❹.

The reason that `Modernizr.load` is called with two different sets of parameters is that the file can accept the following types of arguments: a single file (as a string), an object with name/value pairs, or an array containing a set of either strings or objects. Consequently, we can load in multiple files with a single `Modernizr.load` call. In the first call ❶, we pass in an object with `load` and `complete` properties. (The Modernizr website documents other properties available to use.) At the second call ❹, we only pass in a string. This line

```
Modernizr.load("_js/jquery-1.8.2.min.js");
```

is equivalent to writing

```
Modernizr.load({load : "_js/jquery-1.8.2.min.js"});
```

The first version uses the filename string as a convenient shorthand for loading just that file without any other configuration options.

We also want to load in the game scripts with Modernizr. Create a new file called *game.js* in the *_js* folder. To add the new file to .load, wrap the first Modernizr.load call in array brackets and add a new entry, shown here in bold:

index.html

```
Modernizr.load([{
    load: "//ajax.googleapis.com/ajax/libs/jquery/1.8.2/jquery.js",
    complete: function () {
      if(!window.jQuery){
        Modernizr.load("_js/jquery-1.8.2.min.js");
      }
    },
  },
  {
    load: "_js/game.js"
}]);
```

We can continue adding new files to the Modernizr.load call as new elements in the array at any point before we load *game.js*.

Modernizr will load *game.js*, but the file doesn't contain any code yet. The next task is to set up the main game controller class and run it when loading is complete.

Modular JavaScript

To minimize global variables and the potential for duplicate variable name conflicts, we'll use a modular approach for the JavaScript code. Using a *module* is a way of wrapping all the objects and variables of the game within a single containing namespace. The namespace will be called *BubbleShoot*. A class named Game will be contained within the module BubbleShoot.Game and can be accessed from anywhere else in the application by writing BubbleShoot.Game. This namespace is a safeguard: If we add another JavaScript library later in development that also has a variable named Game, both can exist simultaneously without conflict.

We'll start with the game module, which will run much of the game. Enter the following code into *game.js*:

game.js

```
❶ var BubbleShoot = window.BubbleShoot || {};
❷ BubbleShoot.Game = (function($){
❸   var Game = function(){};
❹   return Game;
❺ })(jQuery);
```

First, we check to see whether the object BubbleShoot exists ❶. Naming our code BubbleShoot.Game is roughly equivalent to using a namespace in languages such as Java or C#. All of the classes will be properties of the BubbleShoot object. Naming collisions aren't likely to happen in small games like *Bubble Shooter* but can become a problem with larger projects. If window.BubbleShoot doesn't exist, it will be created as an empty object. We'll include this line at the top of every class file so we don't have to think about the order in which scripts are loaded.

The next code line defines `BubbleShoot.Game` ❷. This structure—a function inside brackets—may look strange if you're not familiar with it, but it's a common approach to use when you're writing JavaScript modules.

The structure uses an *Immediately Invoked Function Expression (IIFE)*, which is a piece of code that creates a function and runs it immediately. Usually, you will assign the returned results to a variable. The benefit is that the function block creates a variable scope within JavaScript, meaning that any variables created inside it won't pollute the global scope.

The variable declaration contains a function definition followed by parentheses ❺. The function is created, run, and instantly destroyed, but not before returning its contents ❹, which will be the object `Game` created at ❸. The bracket-wrapped function call ❷ is inside the new scope. Once this function has run, we can access the `Game` class from the global scope as `BubbleShoot.Game`.

Now we have a stub of a class, so we need to add some useful code to run. Let's start by hooking up a New Game button. Add the following to *index.html* inside the page div:

index.html

```
<div id="page">
  <div id="top_bar"></div>
  <div id="game"></div>
  <div id="footer_bar"></div>
❶  <div id="start_game" class="dialog">
❷    <div id="start_game_message">
      <h2>Start a new game</h2>
    </div>
❸    <div class="but_start_game button">
      New Game
    </div>
  </div>
</div>
```

The new div elements will create a dialog that displays information to players before they start the game ❶. The dialog will contain a heading with a message ❷ and a New Game button ❸. We still need to add some styling for them to the end of *main.css*, so let's do that now.

main.css

```
.dialog
{
  position: absolute;
  left: 300px;
  top: 110px;
  height: 460px;
  width: 320px;
  background-color: #369;
  border-radius: 30px;
  border: 2px solid #99f;
  padding: 20px 50px;
  color: #fff;
  text-align: center;
  display: none;
```

```
}
.dialog h2
{
  font-size: 28px;
  color: #fff;
  margin: 20px 0 20px;
}
.but_start_game
{
  position: absolute;
  left: 100px;
  top: 360px;
  height: 60px;
  width: 200px;
  background-color: #f00;
  cursor: pointer;
  border-radius: 15px;
  border: 2px solid #f66;
  font-size: 28px;
  line-height: 60px;
  font-weight: bold;
  text-shadow: 0px 1px 1px #f99;
}
.but_start_game:hover
{
  background-color: #f33;
}
#start_game
{
  display: block;
}
```

With this styling in place in *main.css*, reload the page to see the dialog. But note that there's no way for the player to remove it yet. This will happen inside the Game class.

Next, we need some code to run when the page has finished loading so we can attach an event handler to the New Game button. One function will initialize the objects and set up the game after the page has loaded, and another will run every time a new game starts. Make the following changes to *game.js*:

game.js

```
    BubbleShoot.Game = (function($){
      var Game = function(){
❶      this.init = function(){
❷        $(".but_start_game").bind("click",startGame);
        };
❸      var startGame = function(){
        };
      };
      return Game;
    })(jQuery);
```

This new code sets up one public method, called init ❶, and one private method, called startGame ❸. The init method is public because it's attached as a property of the Game object. Inside init, we add a jQuery event handler called bind to the New Game button ❷, which will call the startGame function whenever the button is clicked.

We know the IIFE has a short life and isn't attached as a property of any object, and yet the startGame function can be called here. The reason is due to a JavaScript feature called *closure*. Closure means that a variable exists within the code block that defined it and persists inside that code block. Therefore, the startGame function can be used within other functions inside Game, including init, but can't be accessed by any JavaScript outside of this scope.

We want to call init after the page has loaded, so back in *index.html* we'll add a complete call in Modernizr.load once *game.js* has finished loading:

index.html

```
Modernizr.load([{
    load: "//ajax.googleapis.com/ajax/libs/jquery/1.8.2/jquery.js",
    complete: function(){
      if(!window.jQuery){
        Modernizr.load("_js/jquery-1.8.2.min.js");
      }
    }
  },
  {
    load: "_js/game.js",
    complete: function(){
❶     $(function(){
❷       var game = new BubbleShoot.Game();
❸       game.init();
      })
    }
  }]};
```

Recall that the $ function ❶ is shorthand for the jQuery function, which can do one of several tasks based on what you pass into it. Previously, we've passed in a string (#game), which jQuery interpreted as a selector. In this case, we're passing in a function, which jQuery stores to run once the DOM is ready to be manipulated.

This bit of jQuery functionality is incredibly useful, especially for a game, because from this point we know that we can safely manipulate the DOM with JavaScript even if all of the game's other assets (such as images and sounds) haven't finished loading. Traditionally, client-side interaction has been triggered by waiting for a window.onload event to fire from within JavaScript, which signifies that the HTML has loaded, the DOM is ready, and all of the images are loaded. However, waiting for the images can leave users staring at screens they can't interact with for too long. The preferable alternative is to allow users to interact with the application as soon as the DOM is ready without waiting for the images to load, which produces more responsive interfaces. But determining when the DOM is ready often involves code unique to each browser vendor and frequently changes from one version of a browser to the next. jQuery's $ function smoothes over any browser inconsistencies and lets you achieve that responsiveness without having to determine exactly when the DOM is ready.

Look back at the $ function. Inside it we created an instance of the Game class ❷ and then called the public init method ❸ of that class. Based on what we know about the $ function, anything we do inside init should happen after jQuery has loaded and the DOM is ready for us to work with it.

Now we have an instance of Game that binds its startGame function to the New Game button. However, the startGame function still doesn't do anything. Let's change that!

INTRODUCING CLOSURE

One of JavaScript's most powerful features, *closure* means that variables that have been defined within a function are stored in the function's scope. These variables persist within the scope even when the function has exited, so long as the JavaScript interpreter determines that it still has to make use of them. Reasons for persisting in the scope could include an event handler that requires one of the values when it is triggered or a setTimeout call that will need access to a variable at some time in the future. A simple example will help to explain how this works, but it's worth reading up on closure in order to better make use of it within your own functions.

The following example shows how scope works in JavaScript (and many other languages). The three alert calls in this example should display alerts of 1, 2, and 1 respectively, because the value of myVar inside the function does not overwrite the value in the parent scope. You can run this code from the JavaScript console:

```
var myVar = 1;
alert(myVar);
function innerMyVar(){
  var myVar = 2;
  alert(myVar);
};
innerMyVar();
alert(myVar);
```

To demonstrate how the scope is retained even when a function is executed, we can add a timeout inside the `innerMyVar` function:

```
var myVar = 1;
alert(myVar);
function innerMyVar(){
  var myVar = 2;
  setTimeout(function(){
    alert(myVar);
  },1000);
  myVar++;
};
innerMyVar();
alert(myVar);
```

This code should display alerts of 1, 1, and 3. The scope of `innerMyVar` retains the value of `myVar` defined inside it, including the increment that occurs after the timeout has been defined.

You can read more about scope at *https://developer.mozilla.org/en-US/ docs/Web/JavaScript/Guide/Closures/.*

User Interface and Display Scripts

Let's create a class to handle the user interface and some of the other page display functionality. Create a new file called *ui.js* in the *_js* folder and add the following code:

ui.js

```
var BubbleShoot = window.BubbleShoot || {};
BubbleShoot.ui = (function($){
❶  var ui = {
      init : function(){
      },
❷    hideDialog : function(){
❸      $(".dialog").fadeOut(300);
      }
    };
    return ui;
})(jQuery);
```

Although not much is in this code, notice that the UI object follows the same pattern as the previous Game class. The `hideDialog` function ❷ contains a simple bit of jQuery that fades out any HTML element with the CSS class dialog ❸. The structural difference that ui has from the Game class pattern is that rather than making a ui class, we're just creating a single object ❶ and attaching methods to it. This structure is similar to the way static classes are used in other languages.

The call to fadeOut takes a parameter that specifies the number of milli-seconds to fade out the dialog. We use a value of 300, which is fast enough to not slow down users but not so fast that they won't notice it. The fadeOut method is built into jQuery, but other ways are available to combine selec-tors and manipulate DOM elements. For now, let's quickly run through what jQuery actually does in the fadeOut call:

- Reduces the CSS opacity by a small, fixed amount and repeats in a loop for 300 milliseconds. At the end of this time, the opacity should be zero.
- Sets the display CSS property of the element to none.

We could have created this effect by hand by stringing together some setTimeout calls, but jQuery handles it for us with fadeOut. Using jQuery saves us a lot of code here because, as with many CSS properties, manipulating opacity is not straightforward across browsers (earlier versions of IE use a filter instead of the opacity property, for example).

Note that at the moment we're not doing anything particular to CSS3 or HTML5. We're using old HTML tags and manipulating relatively old CSS properties through JavaScript loops. Later in this book, you'll learn whether you should do this in a more modern way, but for now, the code does the job well. As you develop games, you'll realize that a lot of code runs just as well on earlier browsers as it does on later ones and that, unless you're exclusively rendering to the canvas, your HTML5 games look similar to regular web applications.

Now we need to load our newly created UI file into *index.html* by adding it to the Modernizr.load call:

index.html

```
Modernizr.load([{
    load: "//ajax.googleapis.com/ajax/libs/jquery/1.8.2/jquery.js",
    complete: function(){
      if(!window.jQuery){
        Modernizr.load("_js/jquery-1.8.2.min.js");
      }
    }
  },
❶ "_js/ui.js",
  {
    load: "_js/game.js",
    complete: function(){
      $(function(){
        var game = new BubbleShoot.Game();
        game.init();
      })
    }
  }
]);
```

To add a new *.js* file to the load call ❶, simply add the URL to your script file as an extra array item after *ui.js* but before loading *game.js*. We'll need to add each new script file we create to *index.html*, so remember this process.

To call `hideDialog` when we click the New Game button, add the following lines in bold to *game.js*:

game.js

```
BubbleShoot.Game = (function($){
  var Game = function(){
    this.init = function(){
❶       $(".but_start_game").bind("click",startGame);
    };
    var startGame = function(){
❷       $(".but_start_game").unbind("click");
❸       BubbleShoot.ui.hideDialog();
    };
  };
  return Game;
})(jQuery);
```

Using the `bind` method in jQuery ❶ is a cross-browser way to add event handlers. This method binds a function to an object that triggers when an event occurs. In this game application, the trigger occurs when the user clicks the New Game button, which calls the `startGame` function.

Note that we unbind the event ❷ when the button is clicked to prevent double-clicks from being registered while the button is fading out and trying to start a game twice. If you reload the page and click the New Game button, the dialog should disappear due to the `hideDialog` function ❸.

The *Bubble Shooter* game still doesn't do much, but at least now we have some structure to add code to.

Summary

We now have the foundation in place to start building the game. Modernizr is loading in files, and we can easily add to this task when we create more classes and functions. An instance of the `Game` class is created when the DOM has finished loading, and clicking on a button starts the game.

In the next chapter, we'll create our first sprites for the bubble object, forming the core of the game, and you'll learn how to animate the sprites on the screen.

Further Practice

1. The dialog is being hidden with a jQuery `fadeOut` function, but you can apply other effects to remove the dialog from the screen. Try using `slideUp` or `hide` instead of `fadeOut`, for example. Alternatively, start the dialog offscreen and move it into place with an `animate` call.

2. The colors and styling of the dialogs and the header and footer are quite simple. Change the colors in those areas (or even experiment with graphics) until you find a combination you like.

3. Learn how to use your browser's debugging tools. It's likely you'll have access to breakpoints, watch variables, and the variable stack, so read about and experiment with them. Learning your way around the tools now can be quite a time-saver when you're debugging later. Try adding breakpoints within the `init` and `startGame` functions in *game.js* and trace the code as it runs.

2

SPRITE ANIMATION
USING JQUERY AND CSS

In this chapter we'll dive into moving sprites around the screen. Animation is one of the most common tasks in game development, and the principles you'll learn in animating a simple game apply to most game types.

Although much of the buzz around HTML5 games focuses on the canvas element, you can implement many games just as well using more traditional HTML, CSS, and JavaScript techniques, which are the focus of this chapter. They're useful game development lessons in their own right, and they'll be advantageous when we look into using the canvas element later. Games developed using HTML, JavaScript, and CSS techniques, often referred to as *DOM-based games*, also have much wider browser compatibility. Some older browsers still in use have no canvas support and also are unlikely to support CSS3 transformations and transitions; therefore, we'll use older CSS features.

The key mechanic of the *Bubble Shooter* game is, of course, shooting bubbles, and the bubble that the player fires triggers every bubble-popping effect. We'll start by moving a fired bubble based on user input (a mouse click).

First, we need a way to move a bubble from a starting point A to an ending point B, and that bubble needs to move in a straight line at a constant velocity. Second, we need to determine exactly where points A and B are located. Because the player always fires bubbles from the same position, the starting coordinates (point A) will be the same for each new bubble. Point B will be the coordinates of the user's mouse click when they fire the bubble, so we must retrieve those coordinates. To start, we'll implement that movement from A to B.

In the final game, the bubble won't stop when it reaches the click coordinates but rather will continue until it collides with another bubble or moves off the edge of the screen. We'll deal with collisions later when we more fully develop the game display.

When we have movement from point to point, we can then extrapolate a bubble's path past the user's click and continue to move the bubble forward in the same direction. To find that path, we need to calculate a firing angle based on the relative positions of point A and point B, as shown in Figure 2-1.

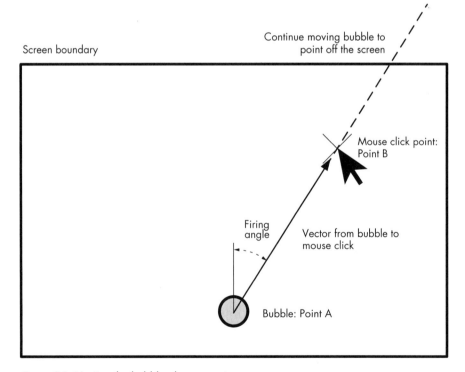

Figure 2-1: Moving the bubble along a vector

Given that firing angle, we can send a bubble in a particular direction as far as needed. Later, we can calculate how far it needs to move by determining any collisions. For now, we'll just define *as far as needed* as a point sufficiently far away to move the bubble off the screen.

Principles of CSS Sprites

A *sprite* is a two-dimensional game element that is part of a larger scene but can move around without affecting the background data. At the moment, the bubble at point A is the only sprite.

At its simplest, in this DOM-based approach, a sprite is an HTML block (often a set of div tags) with CSS styling applied. Due to the way a browser renders HTML, moving a sprite without altering the rest of the screen is easy to do. An HTML element that is absolutely positioned with CSS is rendered independently of the surrounding HTML elements. The browser paints all the objects to the screen and handles layering and overlaps. If we remove an object, the browser knows it needs to display whatever is underneath. This HTML and CSS sprite manipulation property isn't free with canvas development, but as you'll see when we learn more about the canvas element in Chapter 6, it's one of the features that makes DOM game development an ideal place to start and a great tool for rapidly prototyping games.

Creating the Game Board

In the *Bubble Shooter* game, the bubbles will all be sprites so we can move them around the screen as self-contained elements. We'll create the first sprite soon by creating one of the bubbles that will sit in the display. But first we need a container for the game board within the area where all the bubble action happens. We'll put this container in a div called "board", so add the new div to *index.html*:

index.html
```
<div id="game">
  <div id="board"></div>
</div>
```

Next, we'll position the board with CSS. The game board will be centered within the fixed-width display, so we'll make a 760-pixel-wide board and position it 120 pixels from the left edge of the game div, which is positioned to the left of the window. Add the definition for #board to *main.css* after the definition for #game:

main.css
```
body
{
  margin: 0;
}
--snip--
#game
{
```

```
--snip--
}
#board
{
  position: absolute;
  left: 120px;
  top: 0;
  width: 760px;
  height: 620px;
}
```

We also need some CSS to describe a bubble's starting position, width, and height. The player's current bubble will be placed in the bottom center of the play area and will be 50 pixels square. We'll assign the user's current ready-to-fire bubble the CSS class of cur_bubble and define its positioning and appearance in a style sheet. We'll put game elements in their own CSS file so we can easily distinguish them from the various user interface elements, such as dialog boxes and buttons.

Create a new file in the _css directory, call it *game.css*, and put the following code in it:

game.css
```
.bubble
{
  position: absolute;
  width: 50px;
  height: 50px;
}
.cur_bubble
{
  left: 360px;
  top: 470px;
}
```

Each bubble will sit inside a 50-pixel square. We could just fill the game area completely with bubbles, but the trick is to provide a large playing board without making the game too long lasting. After some trial and error, I chose to use 16 bubbles, which should fit in the game area width and still leave a bit of border.

We also need to link *game.css* to the style sheet file in the HTML header, so add that link to *index.html* after the link to *main.css*:

index.html
```
<head>
  <meta charset="UTF-8" />
  <title>Bubble Shooter</title>
  <link href="_css/main.css" rel="stylesheet" />
  <link href="_css/game.css" rel="stylesheet" />
```

The bubble we want to fire doesn't yet display on the screen, so let's add an image to the filesystem and then use some CSS to display it.

Adding Sprites

Figure 2-2 shows how a single bubble will appear (without coloring). The appearance of the bubble will be rendered as a background image within the board div element.

Figure 2-2: Our first bubble sprite graphic

We'll use four different bubble colors, so let's make all four colors of bubbles at the same time. Any four colors will do, as long as they're sufficiently distinct. As with other assets, which are generally images and sound files, we'll store the colored bubbles in an underscored folder. Let's call this one _img.

To speed up loading time and keep file management simple, we'll put the images for all four bubble types into a single PNG file. You can see the complete image in Figure 2-3.

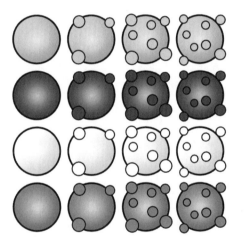

Figure 2-3: A single image file containing all animation states for four bubble types

The PNG file (*bubble_sprite_sheet.png*) contains not only the base state for the four bubbles but also animations of the popping process that we'll use later. The standard bubble image is shown in the left column; the three popping animation stages are shown in the second, third, and fourth columns. Because we have four different bubbles, we'll create CSS definitions that let us display whichever color we want by shifting the position of the background image up or down. The ability to use a single image to render multiple sprites is the reason we're using a CSS background image rather than placing <img> tags directly into the DOM; as a result, the browser needs to download only one image file, which speeds up initialization time. Also, the animation frames for popping are preloaded, so we shouldn't have any nasty pauses while loading images later in the game.

Although we're using four bubble colors, the game doesn't need to know the colors—we might even change the color choices later—but it does need a way to reference them. We'll number the bubble types from zero to three to represent the four colors.

We can use the base CSS class of `.bubble` for properties that are common to all bubbles and add an additional class to the HTML elements when we need to specify the bubble's type (which sets its color). Modify *game.css* as follows:

```css
.bubble
{
  position: absolute;
  width: 50px;
  height: 50px;
  background-image: url("../_img/bubble_sprite_sheet.png");
}
.cur_bubble
{
  left: 360px;
  top: 470px;
}
 .bubble_0
 {
   background-position: 0 0;
 }
 .bubble_1
 {
   background-position: 0 -50px;
 }
 .bubble_2
 {
   background-position: 0 -100px;
 }
 .bubble_3
 {
   background-position: 0 -150px;
 }
```

Now, when we want to render the four bubbles, we can just add the correct classes to a div element, and the background-position property should display the appropriate image. If we want to hard-code a bubble of the last type into the DOM, we'd add the following:

```html
<div class="bubble bubble_3"></div>
```

A bubble of the first type would be

```html
<div class="bubble bubble_0"></div>
```

Although we currently have a definition for the bubble in CSS, we have no HTML to display it on the screen. Instead of hard-coding the bubbles, we'll generate them through JavaScript. But before we start animating a bubble, we need to create and render one, which is the focus of the next section.

Animation and the Bubble Class

Because the bubble is one of the main elements of the game, we'll create a separate JavaScript class for it. We don't yet know all the properties this class might need, but for every bubble object we need to manipulate in code, an onscreen element will display; therefore, we'll create a property to reference that. We'll call it the sprite property, and it will store a reference to the jQuery object that we use to manipulate the DOM element.

Put the following in a separate file called *bubble.js* in the *_js* folder, and add the new file to the Modernizr.load call in *index.html* just after *ui.js*:

bubble.js
```
var BubbleShoot = window.BubbleShoot || {};
BubbleShoot.Bubble = (function($){
  var Bubble = function(sprite){
    var that = this;
❶    this.getSprite = function(){ return sprite;};
  };
❷  Bubble.create = function(){
    var sprite = $(document.createElement("div"));
    sprite.addClass("bubble");
    sprite.addClass("bubble_0");
    var bubble = new Bubble(sprite);
    return bubble;
  };
  return Bubble;
})(jQuery);
```

We have only one argument to pass into the constructor, which is a reference to the jQuery sprite object that will be created within a call to the Bubble.create function ❷. This function currently creates only one type of sprite due to the assigning of the bubble_0 CSS class. Currently, only one method is in the class definition ❶, and it returns the sprite object. When we want to create a bubble, rather than invoking BubbleShoot.Bubble directly, we'll call BubbleShoot.Bubble.create. As a result, we can ensure that all components of a bubble are instantiated correctly and minimize code duplication.

Now we can create Bubble objects, and the document element is created at the same time. However, the bubble still won't be part of the visible DOM because it hasn't been inserted into the document. To handle this, we'll make a function inside Game to create new bubbles and add the CSS class of cur_bubble to the newly created DOM element.

At any time in the game, only a single bubble is on the screen that's ready for the player to fire, so we'll keep a reference to it, called curBubble, in a variable within Game. To finish this step of bubble creation, add the lines in bold to *game.js*:

```
var BubbleShoot = window.BubbleShoot || {};
BubbleShoot.Game = (function($){
  var Game = function(){
❶    var curBubble;
     this.init = function(){
       $(".but_start_game").bind("click",startGame);
     };
     var startGame = function(){
       $(".but_start_game").unbind("click");
       BubbleShoot.ui.hideDialog();
❷       curBubble = getNextBubble();
     };
❸    var getNextBubble = function(){
❹      var bubble = BubbleShoot.Bubble.create();
❺      bubble.getSprite().addClass("cur_bubble");
❻      $("#board").append(bubble.getSprite());
       return bubble;
     };
  };
  return Game;
})(jQuery);
```

At the top of the Game definition, we define curBubble ❶, which will exist only within the scope of the Game object. This empty variable is declared here and is set when the user clicks the New Game button, which calls startGame. Here, curBubble is set to the value returned by getNextBubble ❷. The function getNextBubble ❸ calls BubbleShoot.Bubble.create ❹, which returns an instance of the Bubble class and then adds the CSS class cur_bubble ❺ to the DOM element. Finally, the DOM element is appended to the board div element ❻.

Reload the page and click **New Game**. At the bottom center of the screen you should see a bubble appear. The bubble can't move anywhere yet, but we'll change that in the next section when we add some simple animation.

Calculating Angle and Direction

To determine which direction to fire the bubble in, we need to find out where the mouse is at the moment the user clicks. We can do this by interrogating the event object that will fire in response to the click event. The Game controller needs to know the angle to fire the bubble and what the results of the game display should be. To avoid adding interface code to the controller, the ui object will handle the movement process, which will follow these steps:

1. Find the coordinates of the mouse click.
2. Calculate a vector from the bubble's starting point to the click point.

3. Extend that vector by a sufficient length to move the bubble off the game screen.

4. Move the bubble to the end of the vector.

An example of a bubble's trajectory was shown in Figure 2-1 on page 33. At this point, the movement process assumes that the bubble won't collide with anything, which is the feature we'll tackle first.

In the Game function definition, create the clickGameScreen function (right after the getNextBubble function) and add an event binding to startGame, as shown here:

game.js
```
var BubbleShoot = window.BubbleShoot || {};
BubbleShoot.Game = (function($){
  var Game = function(){
    var curBubble;
    --snip--
    var startGame = function(){
      $(".but_start_game").unbind("click");
      BubbleShoot.ui.hideDialog();
      curBubble = getNextBubble();
      $("#game").bind("click",clickGameScreen);
    };
    --snip--
❶   var clickGameScreen = function(e){
      var angle = BubbleShoot.ui.getBubbleAngle(curBubble.getSprite(),e);
    };
  };
  return Game;
})(jQuery);
```

The function clickGameScreen ❶ will be called in response to the user clicking the screen. As part of the jQuery event handling, it will receive an event object e that contains useful data about the clicked object, including the coordinates of the click. This function also has a call to BubbleShoot.ui.getBubbleAngle, which will calculate a firing angle for the bubble using the event object's click coordinates. The value returned will be an angle, in radians, either to the left or right of the vertical center line of the bubble. Let's write that code now.

In *ui.js*, add the following constant at the top of the ui object and new methods after hideDialog:

ui.js
```
var BubbleShoot = window.BubbleShoot || {};
BubbleShoot.ui = (function($){
  var ui = {
❶   BUBBLE_DIMS : 44,
    init : function(){
    },
    hideDialog : function (){
      $(".dialog").fadeOut(300);
    },
    getMouseCoords : function(e){
❷     var coords = {x : e.pageX, y : e.pageY};
```

```
            return coords;
        },
        getBubbleCoords : function(bubble){
❸         var bubbleCoords = bubble.position();
            bubbleCoords.left += ui.BUBBLE_DIMS/2;
            bubbleCoords.top += ui.BUBBLE_DIMS/2;
            return bubbleCoords;
        },
        getBubbleAngle : function(bubble,e){
            var mouseCoords = ui.getMouseCoords(e);
            var bubbleCoords = ui.getBubbleCoords(bubble);
            var gameCoords = $("#game").position();
            var boardLeft = 120;
❺         var angle = Math.atan((❹mouseCoords.x - bubbleCoords.left - boardLeft)
                / (❹bubbleCoords.top + gameCoords.top - mouseCoords.y));
❻         if(mouseCoords.y > bubbleCoords.top + gameCoords.top){
              angle += Math.PI;
            }
            return angle;
        }
    };
    return ui;
})(jQuery);
```

BUBBLE_DIMS ❶ is the width (and height) of a bubble sprite in the DOM. This constant allows us to calculate the offset to the center of the element, which means we can translate to the (top, left) coordinates that CSS uses. In game programming, you'll often want to work with the center coordinates of an object when you change its position, whereas when rendering, you'll use the (top, left) coordinates.

This new code fetches the coordinates of the player's mouse click ❷ by retrieving two properties that jQuery passes us with the event object e. We also need the starting bubble's coordinates, so the next method ❸ will do that job using another jQuery method. When we have the two coordinate pairs, we can calculate the relative x/y offset between them ❹. Now, we can use the tangent trigonometry function ❺ to calculate the angle based on the x/y offset. Then, if the click is below the center line of the bubble ❻, we add pi (which is 180 degrees, but JavaScript trigonometry is always in radians) to the angle so we can describe a full circle.

To calculate the angle, we've used some trigonometry, which you'll become more familiar with as you build games, if you're not already. The Math.atan method retrieves angles offset from the vertical with positive numbers to the right and negative numbers to the left of vertical. The returned angle will be a value in radians ranging from negative to positive pi.

Firing and Animating Bubbles

Now that we know the angle at which to fire a bubble, we can send it off the screen. Let's assume we'll fire it at 1000 pixels—which is enough to move it outside the game area—and then see the results in action.

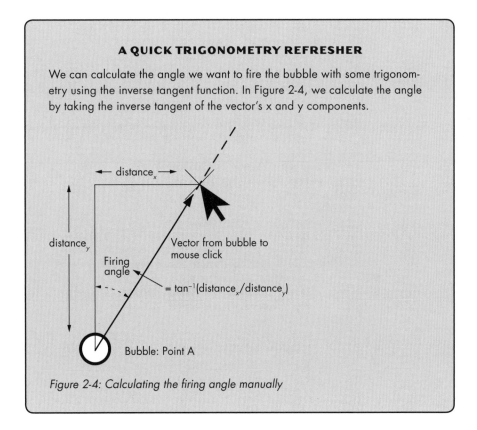
Add the following lines of code to clickGameScreen in *game.js*:

game.js

```
var BubbleShoot = window.BubbleShoot || {};
  BubbleShoot.Game = (function($){
  var Game = function(){
    --snip--
    var clickGameScreen = function(e){
      var angle = BubbleShoot.ui.getBubbleAngle(curBubble.getSprite(),e);
      var duration = 750;
      var distance = 1000;
      var distX = Math.sin(angle) * distance;
      var distY = Math.cos(angle) * distance;
      var bubbleCoords = BubbleShoot.ui.getBubbleCoords(curBubble.
        getSprite());
      var coords = {
        x : bubbleCoords.left + distX,
        y : bubbleCoords.top - distY
      };
❶      BubbleShoot.ui.fireBubble(❷curBubble,❸coords,❹duration);
    };
  };
  return Game;
})(jQuery);
```

The new code sets a duration and total distance, and then calculates the distance along the *x*- and *y*-axes to give coordinates (coords) that are 1000 pixels from its starting point in the direction of the mouse click.

Next, we need to write the fireBubble function ❶ that takes the bubble object ❷, a coordinate to fire at ❸, and a duration ❹ as arguments. We'll put that in the ui class, because it handles just onscreen movement and won't affect the game state.

Add a new method right after getBubbleAngle in *ui.js*:

ui.js
```
var BubbleShoot = window.BubbleShoot || {};
BubbleShoot.ui = (function($){
  var ui = {
    --snip--
    getBubbleAngle : function(bubble,e){
      --snip--
    },
    fireBubble : function(bubble,coords,duration){
      bubble.getSprite().animate({
        left : coords.x - ui.BUBBLE_DIMS/2,
        top : coords.y - ui.BUBBLE_DIMS/2
      },
      {
        duration : duration,
        easing : "linear"
      });
    }
  };
  return ui;
})(jQuery);
```

The fireBubble method is a jQuery call that moves a bubble with jQuery's animate method. The coordinates passed into the function represent the center point of where the bubble needs to stop. To make sure the bubble reaches the correct (top, left) coordinates, fireBubble first translates the coordinates it receives to the top left of the object ❶, which is how CSS positions elements.

The simplest form of animation for moving a sprite around the screen requires two steps: ❶ place the sprite at a fixed position and ❷ move it to a new position a short time later. Repeat the second step until the sprite reaches its destination. With DOM manipulation, we just need to change the top and left CSS properties of the element for each movement and can let the browser take it from there.

We can achieve this animation in two ways. We can use JavaScript animation, which requires us to move the sprite along each step of its path manually, or we can use CSS3 transitions to move the sprite without input from our code each frame. In this chapter, we're focusing on the JavaScript approach; later we'll demonstrate a CSS3 implementation.

As with many of the effects we want to achieve in JavaScript and CSS, we can let jQuery do much of the work for us. The animate method provides a way to animate numerical CSS properties, such as left and top coordinates. It calculates the difference between the start and end values, and it changes the property's values from start to end over a number of steps.

NOTE *This method doesn't work with non-numerical CSS properties because the way to get from start to end can't be calculated easily. For example, you couldn't use* animate *to transition a background color with start and end values that are hexadecimal pairs because interpolating between two colors is not as simple a calculation.*

The animate method takes a number of arguments, including these:

CSS properties ❷   Specifies the properties to animate. Most often, these are positioning properties, such as *top* and *left*, but they could be anything that can be defined by a single-integer dimension in pixels, including font-size, width, height, or even border-width or margin-left. (Note that the shorthand definition for margin, such as margin: 0 10px 20px 10px, contains four different values, so it won't work with animate without being split into the four constituent parts of margin-top, margin-right, margin-bottom, and margin-left.)

Duration ❸   Defines the length in milliseconds of the animation duration. The duration here is fixed at 1 second (1000 milliseconds) for a velocity of 1000 pixels per second. The distance the bubble moves will depend on the game state and, specifically, anything the bubble might collide with. But the duration that we have now should be correct for bubbles that are fired off the screen.

Easing ❹   Defines how an object transitions from its start state to its end state. Easing is usually used to vary acceleration and deceleration along a movement path. For movement, linear results in a constant velocity from start to end, whereas swing adds some starting acceleration and ending deceleration.

You can pass other options to animate as well, and it's worth referring to the jQuery documentation to get an idea of the full potential of the function. To fire the bubble, we need only the preceding parameters.

Reload the page and click in a location above the bubble. The bubble should fly off in that direction. This will work only once. You'll need to refresh the page to see it again, but it's certainly a start.

Summary

In this chapter, you've learned how to perform simple animations with jQuery, HTML, and CSS techniques. Now that we have the basic code in place to move a bubble across the screen in response to a mouse click, it's time to start fleshing out the game.

In Chapter 3, we'll focus on drawing the game board, detecting collisions, and popping bubble groups.

Further Practice

1. If you click in the game area a second time, the bubble appears back on the screen. How would you disable this click event to prevent it?

2. In the .animate call, we specify easing : "linear". Try using "swing" and think about why this may not be appropriate for *Bubble Shooter* but may be a better animation method for other games. Then look at more easing settings at *http://api.jqueryui.com/easings/* and see if you can incorporate any of them into the code.

3

GAME LOGIC

At this point, we've created an intro screen with a New Game button and a single bubble that a player can fire off the screen. In this chapter, we'll turn the *Bubble Shooter* into more of a game. You'll learn how to draw the game board and display the level to the player, and then learn about collision detection.

Collisions are central to many games and happen when sprites touch. Once you can detect collisions, you can write code that makes the sprites react to them. In the *Bubble Shooter*, collisions occur when a fired bubble slams into a bubble in the game grid. We'll implement two reactions: the fired bubble will stick to the board if it doesn't form a color group of three or more bubbles, or it will cause a valid group to fall from the board.

But before we can calculate collisions, we need an object for a bubble to collide with. The first section of this chapter discusses drawing the initial board and setting up the game state. To do so, we'll need to follow a process containing a number of steps, shown in Figure 3-1.

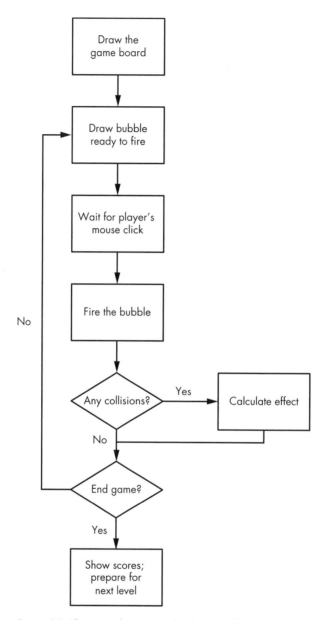

Figure 3-1: The game loop starts by drawing the board and ends by showing the score.

We'll draw the game board first and then add collision detection to the bubble that's been fired. In the next chapter, we'll implement the mechanism to pop groups of bubbles based on matching color.

Let's work through the steps and turn them into code.

Drawing the Game Board

The game board has a similar structure for every level, and each board contains rows of bubbles in four different colors. Alternate rows contain either an odd or even number of bubbles depending on whether the row is odd or even. We'll store all this state information in a Board object and store the current board as a variable in the Game object.

The object structure you choose should vary depending on the game design, but the goals should be the same as when you're deciding how to structure code in web applications: group objects that perform similar operations, and strike a balance with how much common functions are abstracted. Don't define several classes that contain very little code, but don't create too few classes with long code listings that will be difficult to read and understand. Game developers often base initial structural decisions on instinct and experience as well as on hard-and-fast rules. Always be prepared to refactor code if you think your original choices are no longer valid.

The rows that make up the board will be an array of Bubble objects. We'll create this array when we instantiate the Board object. Later, we'll transfer the drawing of the board elements to the DOM from within *ui.js*. Ending up with a large mass of code within a Game class is easy to do but undesirable; therefore, take the opportunity to hand off responsibilities to other classes whenever possible, especially when rendering objects to the screen.

In *game.js*, we need to create a variable to hold the board and a new instance of a Board object. The board is generated when the New Game button is clicked. Add the following new code to *game.js*:

game.js

```
var BubbleShoot = window.BubbleShoot || {};
  BubbleShoot.Game = (function($){
  var Game = function(){
    var curBubble;
    var board;
    --snip--
    var startGame = function(){
      $(".but_start_game").unbind("click");
      BubbleShoot.ui.hideDialog();
      curBubble = getNextBubble();
      board = new BubbleShoot.Board();
      BubbleShoot.ui.drawBoard(board);
      $("#game").bind("click",clickGameScreen);
    };
    --snip--
  };
  return Game;
})(jQuery);
```

Board is a new constructor that we need to make. Create a new file called *board.js* and add it to the list of files to load in `Modernizr.load` in *index.html*. Add the following code to the new file:

board.js

```
var BubbleShoot = window.BubbleShoot || {};
BubbleShoot.Board = (function($){
❶    var NUM_ROWS = 9;
❷    var NUM_COLS = 32;
     var Board = function(){
       var that = this;
❸       var rows = createLayout();
❹       this.getRows = function(){ return rows;};
       return this;
     };
     var createLayout = function(){
       var rows = [];
❺       for(var i=0;i<NUM_ROWS;i++){
         var row = [];
❻         var startCol = i%2 == 0 ? 1 : 0;
         for(var j=startCol;j<NUM_COLS;j+=2){
❼           var bubble = BubbleShoot.Bubble.create(i,j);
           row[j] = bubble;
         };
         rows.push(row);
       };
       return rows;
     };
     return Board;
})(jQuery);
```

NUM_ROWS ❶ and NUM_COLS ❷ are constants that determine the number of rows and columns that make up the bubble board grid. The number of columns may seem high, since we certainly won't have 32 bubbles in a row. The reason for such a large column value is that we'll create a grid entry for every half bubble width, because odd and even rows are offset on the game board. This design decision results in a more visually appealing layout, making it look like bubbles are stacking on top of each other. It also creates more interesting angles for the player to fire at.

All the bubbles on the first row and every subsequent odd row will have odd *y*-coordinates, and those on even rows will have even *y*-coordinates. The rows increment in integer steps, but the array we'll use starts with an index of zero: the first row will be at index 0, the second will be at index 1, and so on. Thus, the bubble coordinates (*x,y*), starting from the top-left corner of the bubble board, will be labeled as shown in Figure 3-2. Specifying coordinates this way and having a half-populated grid avoids having to work with half values and decimal points. In addition, we can store the layout of the board in arrays indexed by integers. Working with integers rather than decimals doesn't change the process we'll follow to calculate collisions, but it does make the code more readable.

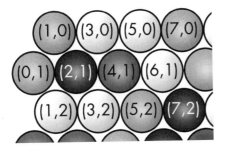

Figure 3-2: Coordinates of the bubbles in the game grid

In the code, we'll now call the createLayout function ❸, which returns a two-dimensional array of rows and columns. We provide public access to this array in the next line ❹. Once we have a Board object, we can retrieve the bubble at any specific row and column position. For example, to access a bubble at coordinate (4,1) we would write:

```
var rows = board.getRows();
var row = rows[1];
var bubble = row[4];
```

Bubbles are accessed by row and then column number. First, we grab all the rows with board.getRows, and then we store the first row from the board as row. Next, we access the fourth bubble within row by its column number. Because the row array is only half populated, all odd entries in even-indexed rows (starting at zero) and all even entries in odd rows will be null.

The createLayout function contains a loop ❺. For each row we want to create, startCol ❻ calculates whether to start on column 1 or 0 depending on whether the row is odd or even, respectively. Then another loop increments to the maximum column number, creates a new Bubble object ❼, and adds it to the row array, which is returned on completion.

For this function to work, we need to adapt the Bubble class to accept row and column input coordinates, and we need to make a change to the Bubble.create method. Also, if a Bubble object knows its position in the grid by storing its coordinates, that information will be useful when we need to calculate groups to pop. When we know a bubble's position, we can access that bubble, as it's stored within the Board object. Then given a bubble, we can interrogate it to determine its position. Each bubble will have a type property, which corresponds to its color, and the property will be determined at creation time.

When you start coding your own game ideas, the decisions about where to store data and how to access it are critical. Your solution will depend on the type of game you're building. In *Bubble Shooter*, we store a relatively small number of Bubbles within a Board object. To find out information about a particular bubble, we can access the data that the Board stores by retrieving data from the rows array.

Depending on how we need to use that bubble data, this method might not be the most elegant solution. For example, imagine we want to find all of the red bubbles in the game. Currently, we would have to loop over every space on the board, check whether the bubble is red, and then store the outcome. The game grid is small, so modern processors can perform this operation quickly. As long as we don't run the color check too many times a second, the current code structure should work.

But now imagine *thousands* of bubbles on the screen. Looping over all the bubbles just to find red ones would consume too much processing power. Instead, we might want to store bubbles in multiple arrays—one for all the red bubbles, one for all the green bubbles, and so on—for instant access to all bubbles of each color. However, there would still be a trade-off: to check whether a given space on the board is occupied by a bubble, regardless of color, we would have to look at multiple arrays.

When you have only a rough sense of how fast a processor can run an operation, it's best to make your code clear and simple. If your game is playable and runs sufficiently fast, you won't need to experiment with different ways to access data. Alternatively, if you identify bottlenecks, you'll then have to refactor some sections to increase their speed. Game development is an iterative process; you'll revisit existing lines of code as much as you write new ones.

How you design objects and where you store their data will vary from game to game. But remember this: if the Game object needs to use that data, one way or another you must allow the object to access it. Whether data is stored directly in a variable or in an array within Game, or is accessed through an intermediate object that Game has access to (such as the Board object in *Bubble Shooter*), the code will need to access that object's state if it needs to make decisions about that object.

To support a bubble storing its position on the board and its color, amend *bubble.js* as follows:

bubble.js

```
var BubbleShoot = window.BubbleShoot || {};
BubbleShoot.Bubble = (function($){
  var Bubble = function(❶row,col,type,sprite){
    var that = this;
    this.getType = function(){ return type;};
    this.getSprite = function(){ return sprite;};
    this.getCol = function(){ return col;};
    this.getRow = function(){ return row;};
  };
  Bubble.create = function(❷rowNum,colNum,type){
❸   if(type === undefined){
❹     type = Math.floor(Math.random() * 4);
    };
    var sprite = $(document.createElement("div"));
    sprite.addClass("bubble");
    sprite.addClass("bubble_" + type);
    var bubble = new Bubble(rowNum,colNum,type,sprite);
    return bubble;
  };
```

```
    return Bubble;
})(jQuery);
```

Bubble now takes grid coordinates and a bubble type as well as the sprite object ❶, where type corresponds to colors that were specified in *game.css*. The Bubble.create method accepts the same parameters ❷; if type isn't passed ❸, one of the four types (colors) is chosen at random ❹.

Now we have a Board object, plenty of bubbles, and their types and positions. But all this information is entirely in memory and is stored within the Board object's rows property. Next, we'll render the level using this information so players can see the game board.

Rendering the Level

Drawing the level is a perfect job for the ui class, because ui represents the game state but doesn't affect that state.

Separating the code that calculates an object's position from the code that renders that object to the screen is a principle you should apply in all of your game ideas. Not only does it separate rendering code from game logic, thereby improving readability, but it also allows you to more easily change how objects are rendered. For example, if the *Bubble Shooter* board was larger and didn't fit on the screen but we wanted to implement a zoom or pan feature, we could change the code that renders the board to either offset the rendering position or to scale up or down to draw a different size board. The power of separating rendering from game logic will become apparent when we switch from DOM-based sprites to drawing onto the HTML canvas element in Chapter 6.

Because the creation of a bubble object involves creating a DOM sprite element, the rendering process needs to place this element in the document and position it correctly. These simple steps follow:

1. Loop over all the rows and columns and pull out each bubble object.
2. Write the bubble's HTML into the DOM.
3. Position the bubble in the correct position.

The next piece of code you add will apply these steps. Open *ui.js*, add a new method (drawBoard) after fireBubble, and then add a new ROW_HEIGHT constant at the top:

ui.js
```
var BubbleShoot = window.BubbleShoot || {};
BubbleShoot.ui = (function($){
  var ui = {
    BUBBLE_DIMS : 44,
    ROW_HEIGHT : 40,
    init : function(){
    },
    fireBubble : function(bubble,coords,duration){
      --snip--
    },
    drawBoard : function(board){
```

```
❶        var rows = board.getRows();
         var gameArea = $("#board");
         for(var i=0;i<rows.length;i++){
           var row = rows[i];
❷          for(var j=0;j<row.length;j++){
             var bubble = row[j];
❸           if(bubble){
❹             var sprite = bubble.getSprite();
❺             gameArea.append(sprite);
              var left = j * ui.BUBBLE_DIMS/2;
              var top = i * ui.ROW_HEIGHT;
❻             sprite.css({
                left : left,
                top : top
              });
            };
          };
        };
      }
    };
    return ui;
})(jQuery);
```

The drawBoard method retrieves the board rows and columns ❶
and loops over them ❷. If there's a bubble ❸ (recall that every other
x-coordinate position is null due to the sparse grid system), drawBoard
grabs the sprite object ❹, appends it to the board ❺, and calculates its
coordinates before setting its position ❻.

To determine a bubble's position, drawBoard first calculates the left coordinate, which is the bubble's column number multiplied by half its width.
To calculate the top coordinate, we'll use a value slightly smaller than the
BUBBLE_DIMS height. The odd and even rows are staggered, and we want the
bubbles to look like they fit together. To create the stacking effect, the vertical separation will be slightly less than the horizontal distance. At the top
of *ui.js*, ROW_HEIGHT has been set to 40, which is 4 pixels less than the height.
This value was determined through trial and error rather than geometrical
calculation: adjust the numbers until the bubble grid looks pleasing to you.

Reload and click **New Game**; you should see a nicely rendered board.
You can even fire a bubble at the rest of the board; unfortunately, it should
just go straight through without hitting anything and continue off the screen
as before.

Because we have only one bubble, we need to refresh to retry the process. Before we begin working on collision detection, we'll make sure we
can keep firing one bubble after another.

The Bubble Queue

Although the player will have only a finite number of bubbles to fire, the
game needs to provide those bubbles in a constant stream. Therefore, we'll
need to add a function that creates a new bubble, adds it to the DOM, and
queues up the next bubble as soon as the user fires the first one.

In *game.js*, add the following variables and functions and change the initialization for curBubble to call a new getNextBubble function:

game.js

```
var BubbleShoot = window.BubbleShoot || {};
BubbleShoot.Game = (function($){
  var Game = function(){
  var curBubble;
  var board;
❶  var numBubbles;
❷  var MAX_BUBBLES = 70;
  this.init = function(){
    $(".but_start_game").bind("click",startGame);
  };
  var startGame = function(){
    $(".but_start_game").unbind("click");
❸    numBubbles = MAX_BUBBLES;
    BubbleShoot.ui.hideDialog();
    curBubble = getNextBubble();
    board = new BubbleShoot.Board();
    BubbleShoot.ui.drawBoard(board);
    $("#game").bind("click",clickGameScreen);
  };
  var getNextBubble = function(){
    var bubble = BubbleShoot.Bubble.create();
    bubble.getSprite().addClass("cur_bubble");
    $("#board").append(bubble.getSprite());
❹    BubbleShoot.ui.drawBubblesRemaining(numBubbles);
    numBubbles--;
    return bubble;
  };
  var clickGameScreen = function(e){
    var angle = BubbleShoot.ui.getBubbleAngle(curBubble .getSprite(),e);
    var duration = 750;
    var distance = 1000;
    var distX = Math.sin(angle) * distance;
    var distY = Math.cos(angle) * distance;
    var bubbleCoords = BubbleShoot.ui.getBubbleCoords(curBubble .getSprite());
    var coords = {
      x : bubbleCoords.left + distX,
      y : bubbleCoords.top - distY
    };
    BubbleShoot.ui.fireBubble(curBubble,coords,duration);
❺    curBubble = getNextBubble();
  };
  return Game;
})(jQuery);
```

The new code first creates a variable ❶ to store the number of bubbles the player has fired. Because the number of fired bubbles is an integer—a basic data type—we'll store it as a variable in Game. If, for example, we had a time limit that a level had to be completed within, we might create an object to store time remaining along with bubbles remaining rather than continuing to create variables in Game. As it is, the variable suits our purpose.

The code also sets a constant for the maximum number of bubbles ❷ the player can fire. When a level is started, it sets the number of bubbles remaining to the value of MAX_BUBBLES ❸ and calls a new function in *ui.js* to display the number of remaining bubbles on the screen ❹. Finally, the code calls getNextBubble ❺ each time a bubble is fired to prepare a new one.

We also want to show the player the number of remaining bubbles available to fire within a level, so create the drawBubblesRemaining method in *ui.js*, appending this new function to the ui object:

ui.js
```
var BubbleShoot = window.BubbleShoot || {};
BubbleShoot.ui = (function($){
  var ui = {
    BUBBLE_DIMS : 44,
    ROW_HEIGHT : 40,
    --snip--
    drawBoard : function(board){
      --snip--
    },
    drawBubblesRemaining : function(numBubbles){
      $("#bubbles_remaining").text(numBubbles);
    }
  };
  return ui;
})(jQuery);
```

Additionally, we need to display the number of remaining bubbles, so add a new element in *index.html*:

index.html
```
<div id="game">
  <div id="board"></div>
  <div id="bubbles_remaining"></div>
</div>
```

Add some styling for the bubbles_remaining div into *main.css*:

main.css
```
#bubbles_remaining
{
  position: absolute;
  left: 479px;
  top: 520px;
  width: 50px;
  font-size: 26px;
  font-weight: bold;
  color: #000;
  text-align: center;
}
```

Now refresh the game. You should be able to fire bubbles into the distance, get a new one as soon as the first is fired (until you've used 70 bubbles, or whatever value you used for MAX_BUBBLES), and be able to fire that new bubble immediately.

Often, you can break down a game into a repeating *turn loop*. The loop is usually initiated by a player action and then closed when that action has been resolved. In *Bubble Shooter*, the loop commences when the player clicks the screen to fire the button and completes when the next bubble is ready to fire. At this point we have the basic turn loop, but to create the game, we need to flesh out the middle part of the loop to calculate where to stop a bubble and whether to pop bubbles.

Detecting Collisions

Although you can now fire bubbles, they pass straight through the board without affecting the bubble grid. The game design calls for them to collide with the board and either become part of the board or cause groups of bubbles that are the same color to pop. The next task is to work out where collisions occur.

We can calculate collisions in two ways:

- Move a sprite forward a few pixels for each frame and then try to detect any overlaps with other sprites. If there's an overlap, we know we've hit another bubble.

- Use geometry to calculate where the sprite might collide with another bubble before it even starts moving.

In fast-paced arcade games, you might choose the first option, as long as there's no chance objects will pass through each other without a collision being detected. These pass-throughs can happen when objects move at high speeds, and collision checks occur after an object has moved numerous pixels since the previous check. For example, in a game in which you fire a bullet at a one-foot-thick wall, the bullet would only be guaranteed to collide with the wall if you check for collisions every foot. If you checked for collisions every two feet instead, you might check for a collision just before the bullet should hit and find no wall. Then two feet further along when you check again, the bullet would be past the wall, again resulting in no collision.

To work around the fast-moving-object problem, we could make sure the steps are always small enough that pass-throughs never happen; however, that requires more calculations, which may not be possible without significant computing power. This problem is more likely to surface in a browser environment: because we never know the specs of the end user's computer, we can't take processing power for granted.

The second option, using geometry, is more accurate if it's feasible. Fortunately, our game design has fairly simplistic geometric properties. Unfortunately, this option isn't possible in games in which sprites have more complex shapes. In that case, you'd have to check whether pixels overlap on a frame-by-frame basis and test thoroughly to ensure you don't see any side effects. For *Bubble Shooter*, we'll use a geometrical approach because we have the following advantages:

- The game is on a regular grid.
- All the objects (the bubbles) are identical.

- We're working in only two dimensions.
- The player moves only one object.
- All the objects are simple geometric shapes (circles), so the calculation of where edges meet is easy.

These conditions make geometric calculations for collisions relatively straightforward. Because game development often involves a lot of geometry, having a good grounding in trigonometry and vectors is essential. The next section discusses the geometry involved in this game. Then we'll turn that geometry into code.

Collision Geometry

When you need to calculate collisions, draw the geometry on a piece of paper before you write the detection code. You'll then be able to visualize the values you'll need to calculate, as shown in Figure 3-3.

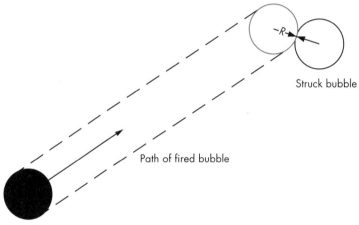

Figure 3-3: Visualizing the geometry behind a bubble collision

The bubble being fired should cause a collision when its center passes within $2R$ (where R is a bubble's radius) of another bubble's center, meaning that the two circumferences are touching. Because the intersection point will always be normal (at 90 degrees) to the colliding bubble's edge and the edge of the bubble being hit, we need to check for a collision only if the path of the moving bubble's center comes within $2R$ of another bubble's center.

To determine where collisions occur, we need to check every other bubble on the board to determine whether the fired bubble's path passes through it. If it overlaps with multiple bubbles, as it does in Figure 3-4, we need to make sure that the struck bubble we pick is the first collision that occurs, which will be the one in which the firing bubble has traveled the least distance.

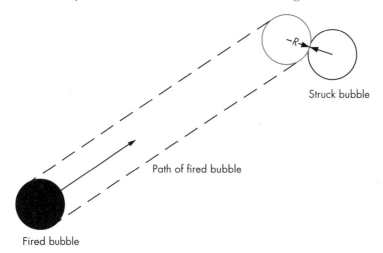

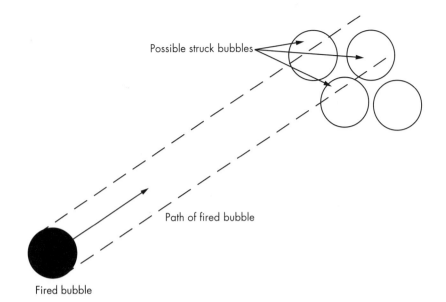

Possible struck bubbles

Path of fired bubble

Fired bubble

Figure 3-4: The fired bubble may be on a path to collide with multiple other bubbles.

Detecting a collision is equivalent to detecting when a vector drawn from the center line of the bubble we're firing intersects with a circle with a radius double that of our bubbles. This will be known as a bubble's *hitbox*. Figure 3-5 shows how we can redraw this concept to help us think about it in a way that's easier to compute.

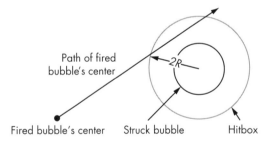

Path of fired bubble's center

$2R$

Fired bubble's center Struck bubble Hitbox

Figure 3-5: If the fired bubble's travel path intersects a stationary bubble's circular hitbox, a collision occurs.

In this diagram, the small filled circle marks the center of the bubble being fired. The bubble it will collide with is the inner circle, and the intersection with the bubble's hitbox (the point marked with the arrow $2R$, which is double a bubble's radius) is where the bubble will stop.

Turning the diagram into a mathematical formula means using vectors. Rather than working through the math before showing any code, let's go straight into the necessary JavaScript, which includes explanatory annotations.

The calculation is a large block of code with a specific function, so we'll put it in its own file. Create a file called *collision-detector.js* and add it to the Modernizr.load call in *index.html*. Type in the following:

collision -detector.js

```
var BubbleShoot = window.BubbleShoot || {};
BubbleShoot.CollisionDetector = (function($){
  var CollisionDetector = {
    findIntersection : function(curBubble,board,angle){
      var rows = board.getRows();
      var collision = null;
      var pos = curBubble.getSprite().position();
      var start = {
        left : pos.left + BubbleShoot.ui.BUBBLE_DIMS/2,
        top : pos.top + BubbleShoot.ui.BUBBLE_DIMS/2
      };
      var dx = Math.sin(angle);
      var dy = -Math.cos(angle);
      for(var i=0;i<rows.length;i++){
        var row = rows[i];
        for(var j=0;j<row.length;j++){
          var bubble = row[j];
          if(bubble){
❶          var coords = bubble.getCoords();
            var distToBubble = {
              x : start.left - coords.left,
              y : start.top - coords.top
            };
            var t = dx * distToBubble.x + dy * distToBubble.y;
            var ex = -t * dx + start.left;
            var ey = -t * dy + start.top;
            var distEC = Math.sqrt((ex - coords.left) * (ex - coords.left) +
              (ey - coords.top) * (ey - coords.top));
            if(distEC<BubbleShoot.ui.BUBBLE_DIMS * .75){
              var dt = Math.sqrt(BubbleShoot.ui.BUBBLE_DIMS * BubbleShoot.
                ui.BUBBLE_DIMS - distEC * distEC);
              var offset1 = {
```

```
        x : (t - dt) * dx,
        y : -(t - dt) * dy
      };
      var offset2 = {
        x : (t + dt) * dx,
        y : -(t + dt) * dy
      };
      var distToCollision1 = Math.sqrt(offset1.x * offset1.x +
        offset1.y * offset1.y);
      var distToCollision2 = Math.sqrt(offset2.x * offset2.x +
        offset2.y * offset2.y);
      if(distToCollision1 < distToCollision2){
        var distToCollision = distToCollision1;
        var dest = {
          x : offset1.x + start.left,
          y : offset1.y + start.top
        };
      }else{
        var distToCollision = distToCollision2;
        var dest = {
          x : -offset2.x + start.left,
          y : offset2.y + start.top
        };
      }
      if(!collision || collision.distToCollision>distToCollision){
        collision = {
          bubble : bubble,
          distToCollision : distToCollision,
          coords : dest
        };
      };
    };
  };
};
  return collision;
}
};
  return CollisionDetector;
})(jQuery);
```

In a moment I'll break down the code in *collision-detector.js*. But
first, notice the call to a new method in *bubble.js* called getCoords ❶, which
returns the center (*x,y*) coordinate of a bubble based on its position in
the row/column hierarchy. You'll need to amend the bubble class to
add the new method:

bubble.js
```
var BubbleShoot = window.BubbleShoot || {};
BubbleShoot.Bubble = (function($){
  var Bubble = function(row,col,type,sprite){
    var that = this;
    this.getType = function(){ return type;};
    this.getSprite = function(){ return sprite;};
    this.getCol = function(){ return col;};
```

```
      this.getRow = function(){ return row;};
      this.getCoords = function(){
        var coords = {
          left : ❶that.getCol() * ❷BubbleShoot.ui.BUBBLE_DIMS/2 +
            ❺BubbleShoot.ui.BUBBLE_DIMS/2,
          top : ❸that.getRow() * ❹BubbleShoot.ui.ROW_HEIGHT +
            ❺BubbleShoot.ui.BUBBLE_DIMS/2
        };
        return coords;
      }
    };
    Bubble.create = function(rowNum,colNum,type){
      --snip--
    };
    return Bubble;
})(jQuery);
```

The game coordinates of a bubble are simple to calculate: you start by finding each top-left corner coordinate. The *x*-coordinate (left) is the column number ❶ multiplied by half the bubble sprite's width ❷. The *y*-coordinate (top) is the row number ❸ multiplied by the row height ❹, which is slightly less than the bubble's full height. To find the center of a bubble, just add half the bubble's dimensions ❺ to both *x* and *y*.

When you're developing game logic, the center coordinates of an object are more often the focus, whereas for rendering purposes, you'll usually specify the top-left corner along with a width and a height. Building a handy method into the object that converts from one to the other will save you from writing out the math each time you need to switch.

Collision Detection Logic

Now let's walk through the entire findIntersection routine in *CollisionDetector .js* block by block. If you don't want to dig into the math right now, you can skip this breakdown—it's purely the math of detecting collisions and doesn't contain any new HTML5 or game development concepts. However, know that in almost every game you write, you'll break down the complexities of how objects interact into a model that you can manipulate with relatively simple mathematics.

Starting Position and Direction Vector

The first part added to *collision-detector.js* is the standard library intro:

```
var BubbleShoot = window.BubbleShoot || {};
BubbleShoot.CollisionDetector = (function($){
  var CollisionDetector = {
```

We've created an object called CollisionDetector. Now let's look at the first method on that object:

```
    findIntersection : function(curBubble,board,angle){
```

When you call `CollisionDetector`, you'll use `BubbleShoot.CollisionDetector`
`.findIntersection`. It accepts the parameters `curBubble` (an instance of the
Bubble class), the board variable (an instance of Board), and the angle at
which the bubble is being fired, giving the function everything it needs
to know about the starting situation.

Now, examine the first variables within `findIntersection`:

```
var rows = board.getRows();
var collision = null;
```

We'll loop over each row to check for collisions, so let's grab the board
rows into a local variable. Assuming there's no collision by default, this will
be the state returned by the function if no intersections occur. As a result,
if the fired bubble doesn't hit another bubble, it will keep moving forward.

The starting value of `collision` is `null` instead of `false` because if an
intersection occurs, it will hold the bubble that's been collided with, plus
some other information, rather than a Boolean that indicates whether or
not a collision has occurred. We need to know that a collision has occurred
(which would be a "true" or "false" result), but more important, we need to
send back information about what was collided with and where the collision
occurred:

```
var pos = curBubble.getSprite().position();
var start = {
  left : pos.left + BubbleShoot.ui.BUBBLE_DIMS/2,
  top : pos.top + BubbleShoot.ui.BUBBLE_DIMS/2
};
```

The next pair of variables retrieves the bubble's starting position (on
the screen) as an object with top and left properties:

```
var dx = Math.sin(angle);
var dy = -Math.cos(angle);
```

Finally, `dx` and `dy` define how much a bubble moves left or right (`dx`) or up
(`dy`) relative to the total distance the bubble will move. With those variables
defined, we can loop through the rows and columns of the game board:

```
for(var i=0;i<rows.length;i++){
  var row = rows[i];
  for(var j=0;j<row.length;j++){
    var bubble = row[j];
    if(bubble){
```

We'll start at the top left of the game board and work our way down and
to the right. Because we only fire bubbles upward, we know that a bubble
will never collide with another from the top of the game board. We also
know that if multiple collision candidates are present along the bubble's
path, we want to grab the one where the bubble has traveled the least

distance—that is, the collision that happened first. Remember that because columns are sparsely populated (every other entry is null), we also need to make sure we're actually looking at a bubble before we try to do anything with it—hence the `if(bubble)` check.

Calculating Collisions

Next we need to use some geometry to check whether the fired bubble's hit-box collided with another bubble. We'll determine where the vector defined by (*dx,dy*), which begins at the center of the fired bubble, intersects with the circle drawn in Figure 3-4. Let's start with the equation of a circle:

$$(x - c_x)^2 + (y - c_y)^2 = r^2$$

Here, *x* and *y* are the points on the circle's circumference, c_x and c_y are the center points of the circle, and *r* is the radius of the circle. We'll need those points to find the distance to the starting bubble.

```
var coords = bubble.getCoords();
var distToBubble = {
  x : start.left - coords.left,
  y : start.top - coords.top
};
```

This part of the loop contains a bubble to check a collision against, so let's get c_x and c_y, the center coordinates of the bubble (coords in the preceding code), and calculate the distance between this point and the fired bubble's coordinates. We don't yet know whether or not a collision will occur.

The bubble being fired follows a set of coordinates defined by the equations:

$$p_x = e_x + td_x$$
$$p_y = e_y + td_y$$

where p_x and p_y are points on the trajectory of the bubble's center point. The calculation of p_x and p_y happens in jQuery's animate method and is the standard equation for moving a point along a line. Next, we'll calculate *t* at the closest point on this line to the center of the bubble that we're checking against:

```
var t = dx * distToBubble.x + dy * distToBubble.y;
```

This line tells us at what proportion of the fired bubble's total movement it will be closest to the candidate bubble's center. From this, we can calculate the screen coordinates where this happens:

```
var ex = -t * dx + start.left;
var ey = -t * dy + start.top;
```

With these coordinates, we can find the distance of *e* (the closest point on the fired bubble's center line to the center of the candidate bubble):

```
var distEC = Math.sqrt((ex - coords.left) * (ex - coords.left) + (ey -
    coords.top) * (ey - coords.top));
```

If the distance `distEC` is less than double the candidate bubble's radius, a collision occurs. If not, the fired bubble will not collide with this candidate bubble.

TRIAL AND ERROR VS. CALCULATION

Note that although `BubbleShoot.ui.BUBBLE_DIMS` gives the width and height of the sprite, we're checking `distEC` against a bubble image that is actually slightly smaller. Multiplying the `BUBBLE_DIMS` value by 0.75 (obtained from a bit of trial and error) gives a diameter for a bubble that works in the game.

We can arrive at a more precise value for `distEC` by measuring the width of the bubble, which is 44 pixels in the images in this book. Dividing by the `BUBBLE_DIMS` of 50 pixels, the result is a multiplier of 0.88. Although this larger value might be more exact, it requires the player to be more accurate when trying to fire bubbles through gaps. Therefore, 0.75 just feels better to the player, because it gives them more chances to make shots that they would find very difficult if the math were precise.

Often in game development, you'll make decisions based on trial and error as much as by calculation. In this case, by using a slightly smaller value, you give the player the opportunity to fire bubbles through small gaps in the game board. Players won't notice the lax enforcement of the laws of physics, and they'll enjoy the game more.

If `distEC` is less than three-quarters of the bubble sprite width, we know that the fired bubble's travel path intersects the candidate bubble's hitbox at some point:

```
if(distEC < BubbleShoot.ui.BUBBLE_DIMS * .75){
```

Most likely, a second intersection point will occur where the line exits the bubble's hitbox (see Figure 3-5, which shows the center line of the fired bubble passing through the hitbox at two points), but we only want the first. Two calculations will ensure that we have the correct intersection. Let's look at the first calculation:

```
var dt = Math.sqrt(BubbleShoot.ui.BUBBLE_DIMS * BubbleShoot.ui.BUBBLE_DIMS
    - distEC * distEC);
```

Here, we find the distance between the center of the struck bubble and the closest point on the fired bubble's path. The second calculation follows:

```
var offset1 = {
  x : (t - dt) * dx,
  y : -(t - dt) * dy
};
var offset2 = {
  x : (t + dt) * dx,
  y : -(t + dt) * dy
};
```

The points on the line that cross the stationary bubble's center are calculated here as offsets from the fired bubble's path at point t.

Finding the Correct Collision Point

Now we want to choose which intersection we'll encounter first—that is, which point is closest to where we're firing curBubble from—so we need the distances to each potential collision point:

```
var distToCenter1 = Math.sqrt(offset1.x * offset1.x + offset1.y *
  offset1.y);
var distToCenter2 = Math.sqrt(offset2.x * offset2.x + offset2.y *
  offset2.y);
```

Next, we'll choose the correct collision point and calculate where curBubble needs to stop by adding the starting coordinates back into the system:

```
if(distToCollision1 < distToCollision2){
  var distToCollision = distToCollision1;
  var dest = {
    x : offset1.x + start.left,
    y : offset1.y + start.top
  };
}else{
  var distToCollision = distToCollision2;
  var dest = {
    x : -offset2.x + start.left,
    y : offset2.y + start.top
  };
}
```

Most of the time, if the center of the bubble being fired collides with the edge of another bubble, it'll cross twice: once on the way in and once on the way out. In the rare cases where it just brushes past and only a single collision point occurs, we'll get two identical results, so it doesn't matter which one we choose.

At this point, the function will loop over every bubble in the display and check for collisions; however, we don't want to know about *every* collision—just the *nearest* one that occurs earliest in curBubble's movement path.

To store the current best-match collision, we use the collision variable, which was set to null before the loop started. Then, each time we find a collision, we check to see if the new collision is closer than the previous best. If no previous collision happened, the first one we find will be the best. The collision object stores a reference to the stationary bubble that the fired bubble collides with, the distance to the collision, and the coordinates where it happened:

```
            if(!collision || collision.distToCollision>distToCollision){
                collision = {
                  bubble : bubble,
                  distToCollision : distToCollision,
                  coords : dest
                };
              };
            };
          }
        }
    };
    return collision;
};
```

Now the findIntersection function will return an object with all the data we need if a collision is found or null if no collision occurs. All of these calculations happen before the bubble has even started moving.

Reacting to Collisions

We now need to use the collision coordinates we have in an amended version of clickGameScreen in *game.js* so we can fire and stop bubbles. We've written the first step in detecting a collision by resolving what the bubble has collided with (which may be *nothing*!). Now, Game needs to decide how to react to that information.

First, we check for a collision. If one occurs, we move the bubble to wherever the collision occurred. If one doesn't occur, we fire the bubble off the screen. Change the existing clickGameScreen function in *game.js* to the following:

game.js
```
var clickGameScreen = function(e){
    var angle = getBubbleAngle(e);
    var bubble = $("#bubble");
    var duration = 750;
    var distance = 1000;
    var collision = BubbleShoot.CollisionDetector.findIntersection(curBubble,
      board,angle);
    if(collision){
      var coords = collision.coords;
```

```
❶      duration = Math.round(duration * collision.distToCollision / distance);
    }else{
      var distX = Math.sin(angle) * distance;
      var distY = Math.cos(angle) * distance;
      var bubbleCoords = BubbleShoot.ui.getBubbleCoords(curBubble.getSprite());
      var coords = {
        x : bubbleCoords.left + distX,
        y : bubbleCoords.top - distY
      };
    };
    BubbleShoot.ui.fireBubble(curBubble,coords,duration);
    curBubble = getNextBubble();
  };
```

If the distance the bubble moves has changed due to a collision, the time it needs to get there should also change, so all bubbles fire at the same velocity. We'll use the collision data to recalculate that duration ❶.

Reload the game and fire a bubble. The bubble should stop when it hits the main group. But it still doesn't look quite right. The bubble stops, but it doesn't integrate itself into the board. It just sticks wherever it hits. Also, if you fire more bubbles, they just pile on top of each other; new bubbles won't collide with previously fired bubbles. The problem is that the board state doesn't change to synchronize with the display state, so we'll correct this using two steps:

1. Add the fired bubble to the board state in the correct row and column.

2. When the fired bubble stops, lock it into a tidy grid position.

The second step will use information from the first.

Adding the bubble Object to the Board

The bubble object, curBubble, is in the DOM and should end up close to the correct position on the screen, so we can add it to the board's row/column array when we know where it should fit.

To calculate the row number, we divide the y-coordinate by the height of rows and round down the result. Calculating the column number is similar, except we need to snap to either odd column numbers on even rows (including zero) or even column numbers on odd rows. Finally, we can add the bubble to the rows property of the Board object, because Board is where we're storing positional information for all of the bubbles.

The function to add the fired bubble is trivial, so we'll put that in *board.js*. Within the definition of the board class and after the getRows method, add the following:

board.js
```
var BubbleShoot = window.BubbleShoot || {};
BubbleShoot.Board = (function($){
  var NUM_ROWS = 9;
  var NUM_COLS = 32;
  var Board = function(){
    var that = this;
```

```
            var rows = createLayout();
            this.getRows = function(){ return rows;};
            this.addBubble = function(bubble,coords){
              var rowNum = Math.floor(coords.y / BubbleShoot.ui.ROW_HEIGHT);
              var colNum = coords.x / BubbleShoot.ui.BUBBLE_DIMS * 2;
              if(rowNum % 2 == 1)
                colNum -= 1;
              colNum = Math.round(colNum/2) * 2;
              if(rowNum % 2 == 0)
                colNum -= 1;
              if(!rows[rowNum])
                rows[rowNum] = [];
❶            rows[rowNum][colNum] = bubble;
❷            bubble.setRow(rowNum);
❸            bubble.setCol(colNum);
            };
            return this;
          };
          var createLayout = function(){
            --snip--
          };
          return Board;
        })(jQuery);
```

Note that as well as adding the bubble into the correct row-column position in rows[][] ❶, we're also passing the calculated row ❷ and column ❸ numbers to the bubble object so it knows its location relative to the other bubbles. We don't have those method calls yet, so let's create them now in *bubble.js* in the Bubble class definition:

bubble.js
```
var Bubble = function(row,col,type,sprite){
  var that = this;
  this.getType = function(){ return type;};
  this.getSprite = function(){ return sprite;};
  this.getCol = function(){ return col;};
  this.setCol = function(colIn){ col = colIn;};
  this.getRow = function(){ return row;};
  this.setRow = function(rowIn){ row = rowIn;};
  this.getCoords = function(){
    --snip--
  }
};
```

Next, amend *game.js* to call this new method in clickGameScreen:

game.js
```
var clickGameScreen = function(e){
  var angle = BubbleShoot.ui.getBubbleAngle(curBubble.getSprite(),e);
  var duration = 750;
  var distance = 1000;
  var collision = BubbleShoot.CollisionDetector.findIntersection(curBubble,
    board,angle);
  if(collision){
    var coords = collision.coords;
```

```
      duration = Math.round(duration * collision.distToCollision / distance);
      board.addBubble(curBubble,coords);
    }else{
      var distX = Math.sin(angle) * distance;
      var distY = Math.cos(angle) * distance;
      var bubbleCoords = BubbleShoot.ui.getBubbleCoords(curBubble.getSprite());
      var coords = {
        x : bubbleCoords.left + distX,
        y : bubbleCoords.top - distY
      };
    };
    BubbleShoot.ui.fireBubble(curBubble,coords,duration);
    curBubble = getNextBubble();
};
```

Reload the game and shoot a few bubbles. They should start to pile up, although some may still overlap because they don't quite settle properly into the grid. It's progress, but we want the bubbles to line up nicely when they collide—that's what we'll do next.

Locking the bubble Object into the Grid

When the fired bubbles collide with the rest of the board, we want to lock them in place rather than just having them stop wherever they hit. The current movement works well, but we need to add another step that locks the bubble into position when it reaches its destination.

After board.addBubble has been run, the bubble object knows which row and column it's located in; therefore, calling its getCoords method (which calculates based on row and column) will retrieve the coordinates where it should be rather than the coordinates where it actually stopped. To nudge it into place, we'll add a complete function that can be set as part of a jQuery animate call and use the information the bubble already has. As a result, we can fire the bubble and forget about it rather than creating a process to tidy up bubbles as they land. jQuery's complete callback function is a useful place to put code that needs to run when an animation has finished. For example, in a game with an explosion effect, the frames of the animation could run, and when the animation finishes, the DOM elements that formed the explosion could be removed from the screen.

The complete property is called when the animation has ended. In *ui.js* amend fireBubble as follows:

ui.js
```
fireBubble : function(bubble,coords,duration){
  bubble.getSprite().animate({
      left : coords.x - ui.BUBBLE_DIMS/2,
      top : coords.y - ui.BUBBLE_DIMS/2
    },
    {
      duration : duration,
      easing : "linear",
      complete : function(){
❶       if(bubble.getRow() !== null){
```

```
          bubble.getSprite().css({
            left : bubble.getCoords().left - ui.BUBBLE_DIMS/2,
            top : bubble.getCoords().top - ui.BUBBLE_DIMS/2
          });
        };
    }
  });
},
```

When you reload, the bubbles you fire should settle into the grid system. Note that we use getRow to check whether a collision has occurred ❶, because getRow should return null for a bubble that misses all other bubbles and moves off the screen.

Summary

Now that fired bubbles collide with the others on the board, *Bubble Shooter* is starting to act more like a game. We've moved sprites across the screen using jQuery, made the game react to the player's input, and set up some of the basic game logic. However, currently there's no way to pop bubbles, and it won't be much of a game without that functionality. Popping logic and displaying an animation are the subjects of the next chapter.

Further Practice

1. Each row of the game board is offset to form a staggered pattern. Change the code in createLayout so the bubbles form a regular grid. How will this change the game?

2. Now that you can make createLayout build a different grid pattern, write code to generate an entirely new layout. For example, you could draw only every alternate column or build a more creative layout.

3. *Bubble Shooter* has a simple object structure that consists of a Game, a Board, and a set of Bubbles. What sort of objects would you need if you were building a game like *Angry Birds*, *Bejeweled*, or *Candy Crush*?

4

TRANSLATING GAME STATE CHANGES TO THE DISPLAY

 Animation is a powerful visual cue to show players how their actions affect a game. Whenever a player causes the game state to change, you need to display the results. In this chapter, you'll add code to detect and remove bubble groups, learn more about animating CSS sprites, and implement a nifty exploding effect in jQuery.

At this point, players can fire bubbles at the game board, and those bubbles will become part of the bubble grid. Now, we need to pop groups of matching bubbles when a player fires the correct color at them. When curBubble is fired into another bubble and a group of three or more matching bubbles forms, all bubbles in that group should show a popping animation and then be removed from the display and the Board object.

We'll also need to detect and handle any cascading effects caused by popping bubbles. For example, if sets of bubbles are disconnected from the main group when we pop another set, we should destroy the disconnected bubbles in a different way.

Calculating Groups

The Board object contains the row and column information for each bubble in the grid and will determine whether a fired bubble forms a group of three or more when it lands. We'll add a function to *board.js* that returns all of the bubbles surrounding a given (row,column) position. Then we'll group them by color and work out which ones to pop.

Fetching Bubbles

First, we need to retrieve the set of bubbles surrounding the specified coordinates from the board's rows variable. Add the following methods to *board.js* after the addBubble method:

board.js

```
var Board = function(){
  var that = this;
  var rows = createLayout();
  this.getRows = function(){ return rows;};
  this.addBubble = function(bubble,coords){
    --snip--
  };
❶ this.getBubbleAt = function(rowNum,colNum){
    if(!this.getRows()[rowNum])
      return null;
    return this.getRows()[rowNum][colNum];
  };
❷ this.getBubblesAround = function(curRow,curCol){
    var bubbles = [];
    for(var rowNum = curRow - 1;rowNum <= curRow+1; rowNum++){
      for(var colNum = ❸curCol-2; colNum <= ❹curCol+2; colNum++){
        var bubbleAt = that.getBubbleAt(rowNum,colNum);
        if(bubbleAt && !(colNum == curCol && rowNum == curRow))
❺        bubbles.push(bubbleAt);
      };
    };
    return bubbles;
  };
  return this;
}
```

The getBubbleAt method ❶ takes an input row and column coordinate and returns the bubble at that location. If no bubble exists at that location, it returns null. The getBubblesAround method ❷ loops through the three relevant rows—the same row, the one above, and the one below—and then examines the surrounding columns, calling getBubbleAt for each position. Note that getBubbleAt returns null for every alternate column entry due to the half-populated row arrays. For this reason, we look at two entries to the left ❸ (curCol-2) and two to the right ❹ (curCol+2) of the current bubble. No matter whether we start on an odd or an even row, this method should work. We also need to check that a bubble exists at the coordinates we're examining and that we don't add the bubble that we're checking around ❺.

Any bubbles surrounding the fired bubble are pushed into the bubbles array and are returned by getBubblesAround. Each bubble stores its own coordinates, so we don't need to sort the array or store position information separately.

Creating Matching Color Groups

Next, we'll write a more substantial function called getGroup to return groups that are the same color as the first bubble and are connected to that bubble. This recursive function will accept two parameters: a bubble, which sets the starting coordinates and the color (type) definition, and an object, which stores bubbles that are part of the group. The object will store found bubbles in two arrays added as properties: first as a linear array and additionally in an array indexed by row and column. The second array allows us to easily check whether we have already added a bubble to the matching set to avoid adding duplicates. Both arrays are added as properties of an object so we can return both when we call the method. The flowchart in Figure 4-1 shows an overview of this process.

The function we'll add to the Board class looks like this:

board.js

```
var Board = function(){
  var that = this;
  var rows = createLayout();
  this.getRows = function(){ return rows;};
  this.addBubble = function(bubble,coords){
    --snip--
  };
  this.getBubbleAt = function(rowNum,colNum){
    --snip--
  };
  this.getBubblesAround = function(curRow,curCol){
    --snip--
  };
  this.getGroup = function(bubble,found){
    var curRow = bubble.getRow();
    if(!found[curRow])
      found[curRow] = {};
    if(!found.list)
      found.list = [];
    if(found[curRow][bubble.getCol()]){
      return found;
    }
    found[curRow][bubble.getCol()] = bubble;
    found.list.push(bubble);
    var curCol = bubble.getCol();
    var surrounding = that.getBubblesAround(curRow,curCol);
    for(var i=0;i<surrounding.length;i++){
      var bubbleAt = surrounding[i];
      if(bubbleAt.getType() == bubble.getType()){
        found = that.getGroup(bubbleAt,found);
      };
    };
  };
```

```
    return found;
  };
  return this;
};
```

Let's break down this new function and walk through the logic. After we pass in the `bubble` object and `found` object, `getGroup` first checks to see if this bubble was already found.

```
    var curRow = bubble.getRow();
❶  if(!found[curRow])
      found[curRow] = {};
❷  if(!found.list)
      found.list = [];
❸  if(found[curRow][bubble.getCol()]){
      return found;
    }
❹  found[curRow][bubble.getCol()] = bubble;
❺  found.list.push(bubble);
```

If the bubble was already found, `getGroup` should return the current unchanged data and stop. If the `found` object doesn't have an entry for the current row, we need to create an empty array ❶. Then, if the `list` property doesn't exist, it needs to be created ❷ but only on the initial call to the function. If this bubble was detected previously, we return the found object without adding the bubble again ❸. Otherwise, we track that we've looked in this location ❹ and store the bubble in the `found` list ❺.

Next, we retrieve the surrounding bubbles ❻.

```
    var curCol = bubble.getCol();
❻  var surrounding = that.getBubblesAround(curRow,curCol);
```

At most, there should be six, and then we need to check each for a color match:

```
  for(var i=0;i<surrounding.length;i++){
    var bubbleAt = surrounding[i];
❼  if(bubbleAt.getType() == bubble.getType()){
      found = that.getGroup(bubbleAt,found);
    };
  };
❽ return found;
```

If a bubble matches the fired bubble's color ❼, the function calls itself; `getGroup` adds the checked bubble to the flat array and marks that its coordinates have been checked. The function calls itself again, passing in the newly found bubble and the current data state (with the `found` list). Whatever the result, we'll return the final value of `found` ❽.

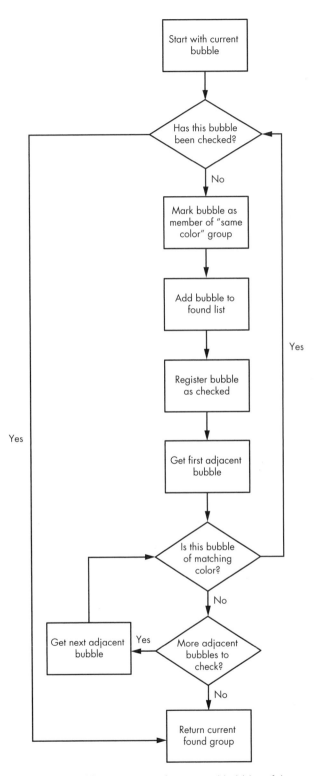

Figure 4-1: Grabbing a group of connected bubbles of the same color

Now we need to call this method when the bubble is fired. In *game.js,*
add in the clickGameScreen routine:

game.js

```
var clickGameScreen = function(e){
  var angle = BubbleShoot.ui.getBubbleAngle(curBubble.getSprite(),e);
  var duration = 750;
  var distance = 1000;
  var collision = BubbleShoot.CollisionDetector.findIntersection(curBubble,
    board,angle);
  if(collision){
    var coords = {
      x : bubbleCoords.left + distX,
      y : bubbleCoords.top - distY
    };
    duration = Math.round(duration * collision.distToCollision / distance);
    board.addBubble(curBubble,coords);
❶   var group = board.getGroup(curBubble,{});
❷   if(group.list.length >= 3){
❸     popBubbles(group.list,duration);
    }
  }else{
    --snip--
  };
  BubbleShoot.ui.fireBubble(curBubble,coords,duration);
  curBubble = getNextBubble();
};
```

When we fetch a group of bubbles with board.getGroup ❶, we might end
up with a group containing fewer than three bubbles. Because we need
to consider only groups of three or more bubbles, we'll skip any smaller
groups ❷. Now we just need to write the routine for popping bubbles ❸!

Popping Bubbles

We need the game to determine whether a group of bubbles has three
or more bubbles, and if so, remove those bubbles. In this section, you'll
implement the JavaScript functions that remove bubble groups and add a
fun popping animation with CSS.

Removing Bubble Groups with JavaScript

We'll begin by calculating what the board should look like after a group has
been popped. When that's complete, we can update the display and remove
any popped bubbles from view. As long as the game state is calculated correctly, you can add animation thereafter. Updating the game state and then
writing separate code to display the new state is a useful approach to take
throughout game development.

Add a new function called `popBubbles` after `clickGameScreen`:

game.js

```
var BubbleShoot = window.BubbleShoot || {};
BubbleShoot.Game = (function($){
  var Game = function(){
    --snip--
    var clickGameScreen = function(e){
      --snip--
    };
    var popBubbles = function(bubbles,delay){
❶    $.each(bubbles,function(){
        var bubble = this;
❷      board.popBubbleAt(this.getRow(),this.getCol());
        setTimeout(function(){
          bubble.getSprite().remove();
        },delay + 200);
      });
    };
  };
  return Game;
})(jQuery);
```

The popBubbles function loops over each `bubble` object in the array we pass it ❶ and tells the board to remove the bubble ❷ by calling `popBubbleAt` (which we'll write next). Then it waits for `delay + 200` milliseconds to remove the bubble from the DOM to allow time for the animation of firing the bubble to run. As a result, the user can see what's happened before the screen is updated. The starting value of `delay` is passed in from the fired bubble's duration—the time it took to travel from its starting point—so bubbles will always disappear 200 milliseconds after the grouping has occurred.

The final piece of code is in *board.js*, where we need to define `popBubbleAt`. Add the following method after the close of the `getGroup` method:

board.js

```
var Board = function(){
  --snip--
  this.getGroup = function(bubble,found){
    --snip--
  };
  this.popBubbleAt = function(rowNum,colNum){
    var row = rows[rowNum];
    delete row[colNum];
  };
  return this;
};
```

The popBubbleAt method simply removes the entry you pass it from the row/column array.

Reload the game and fire a bubble. When you make a set of three or more bubbles, they should disappear from view. At last, *Bubble Shooter* is starting to look more like a game!

Popping Animations with CSS

Moving sprites around the screen with CSS is one type of animation, but now it's time to animate sprites in a different way and change how they *look*. This will present players with a visually rewarding popping animation, which will use the other sprite frames we created at the beginning of the book.

The best way to animate a sprite graphic is by changing the position of its background image. Recall that *bubble_sprite_sheet.png* (shown again in Figure 4-2 for convenience) contains not only the four bubble types but also four different states for each color.

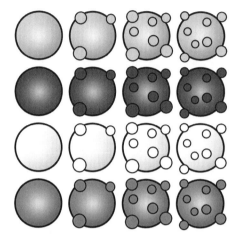

Figure 4-2: The four states of the bubble sprite,
as contained in bubble_sprite_sheet.png

We can display a popping animation by showing the four frames in succession, which we'll do by shifting the background image to the left by 50 pixels at a time.

The game pops only bubbles in groups, but the popping effect won't be nearly as fun to watch if all the bubbles in a group disappear at once. To make the effect more interesting, we'll pop the bubbles individually rather than all together. Doing so will require a small change to the popBubbles method we just added to *game.js*:

game.js

```
var popBubbles = function(bubbles,delay){
  $.each(bubbles,function(){
    var bubble = this;
    setTimeout(function(){
❶    bubble.animatePop();
    },delay);
    board.popBubbleAt(bubble.getRow(),bubble.getCol());
    setTimeout(function(){
      bubble.getSprite().remove();
    },delay + 200);
❷  delay += 60;
  });
};
```

Here, we call `animatePop` ❶, a new method that we'll add to `Bubble` to change the bubble's background image position. The first bubble's popping animation should start as soon as the fired bubble collides with it. But subsequent pops should be delayed by 60 milliseconds by incrementing `delay` ❷. Add `animatePop` to *bubble.js*.

bubble.js

```
var Bubble = function(row,col,type,sprite){
  --snip--
  this.getCoords = function(){
  --snip--
  };
  this.animatePop = function(){
❶    var top = type * that.getSprite().height();
❷    this.getSprite().css(Modernizr.prefixed("transform"),"rotate(" + (Math.
       random() * 360) + "deg)");
❸    setTimeout(function(){
       that.getSprite().css("background-position","-50px -" + top + "px");
     },125);
     setTimeout(function(){
       that.getSprite().css("background-position","-100px -" + top + "px");
     },150);
     setTimeout(function(){
       that.getSprite().css("background-position","-150px -" + top + "px");
     },175);
❹    setTimeout(function(){
       that.getSprite().remove();
     },200);
  };
};
```

Based on the bubble's type, `animatePop` calculates ❶ the value representing the top part of the bubble's `background-position` property. The type value tells us what color the bubble should be; we'll use it to select the appropriate row of popping animation images. Next, using a basic CSS transformation, we add a bit of visual variation ❷ to the animation by rotating the bubble sprite at a random angle to prevent all the popping animations from appearing identical. You'll see more examples of CSS transformations in Chapter 5. To stagger the start time of each popping animation, the function makes three delayed calls ❸ that move the `background-position` to the left by 50 pixels.

NOTE *Hard-coding an animation this way is not very scalable, but* Bubble Shooter *has only one sprite with three frames to display. Therefore, we can avoid writing a generic function, which is the reason we use a sequence of* setTimeout *calls instead. When we implement the same animation using* canvas *rendering, you'll see an example of how to code an animation that is more reusable.*

Finally, `animatePop` removes the sprite's DOM element ❹ when the animation has finished. Removing the node from the DOM helps with memory management, which would be even more important in a game with more onscreen objects. At approximately 20 frames per second, the resulting animation frame rate is fairly poor. A professional game should have a frame rate of three times that number. But the principle of creating an animation by shifting a background image is the same regardless.

When you reload the page and fire a bubble to make a matching group, you should see a pleasing popping animation. However, after popping numerous bubbles, you may see a side effect of removing bubbles that we need to remedy: a popped group might be the only element holding a set of bubbles of varied colors onto the main board. Currently, these bubbles are left hanging in space and look a bit odd. Because the game design stipulates that these bubbles be removed as well, we'll do that next.

Orphaned Groups

Groups of bubbles that have been disconnected from the rest of the board are called *orphans*. For example, in Figure 4-3, popping the boxed group of bubbles would leave four orphaned bubbles hanging in midair. Orphaned sets of bubbles need to be removed by the firing bubble as well. But rather than have them pop in the same way as popped groups, we'll add a different animation. Orphans will fall off the screen and appear as though they were hanging and had their supports cut. Not only will players recognize that something different has happened, but we also get to experiment with a different animation type. Currently, detecting orphaned groups is not part of the code; so, before we can animate them, we need to find them.

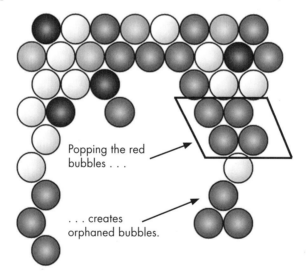

Popping the red bubbles . . .

. . . creates orphaned bubbles.

Figure 4-3: Popping the red bubbles creates four orphaned bubbles.

Identifying Orphaned Bubbles

We'll check each bubble and determine whether it's part of a group that's connected to any bubbles in the top row. Because the top row is considered to be permanently attached, any bubble that can't trace a route back to the top row will be identified as part of an orphaned group.

Tracing this route might seem like a problem we haven't encountered yet; however, we can actually use the already written getGroup method and find orphaned sets quite simply. Figure 4-4 shows the process for checking whether a group is part of an orphaned set.

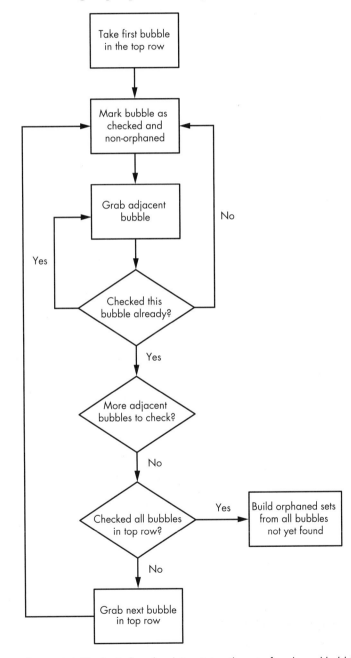

Figure 4-4: The logic flow for determining the set of orphaned bubbles

Using this logic, we can reuse the getGroup function in step 2. But to do so, we need to revise the criterion that bubbles must be the same color to form a group.

Let's change getGroup to take a parameter that allows for the selection of nonmatching color groups:

board.js

```
var Board = function(){
  --snip--
❶  this.getGroup = function(bubble,found,differentColor){
    var curRow = bubble.getRow();
    if(!found[curRow])
      found[curRow] = {};
    if(!found.list)
      found.list = [];
    if(found[curRow][bubble.getCol()]){
      return found;
    }
    found[curRow][bubble.getCol()] = bubble;
    found.list.push(bubble);
    var curCol = bubble.getCol();
    var surrounding = that.getBubblesAround(curRow,curCol);
    for(var i=0;i<surrounding.length;i++){
      var bubbleAt = surrounding[i];
❷    if(bubbleAt.getType() == bubble.getType() || differentColor){
        found = that.getGroup(bubbleAt,found,differentColor);
      };
    };
    return found;
  };
}
```

The function definition now takes an extra parameter ❶. Where getGroup is called recursively, it should ignore the type check ❷ if the value is set to true, and it passes the input parameter through the recursion chain. With these simple changes, a getGroup(bubble,{},true) call should return all bubbles that the passed bubble is connected to regardless of color. Calling getGroup(bubble,{},false) or just getGroup(bubble,{}) should operate the same way as before.

The findOrphans function will be a method in the Board class and will examine every bubble in the top row, finding the group of bubbles each one connects to. (Initially, every bubble on the board will be in one big group, except the bubble to be fired.) An array of (row,column) values will be populated with false values, and every time a bubble is found, the (row,column) entry will be set to true for that location. At the end of the process, coordinates that contain a bubble but have a value set to false in the returned array will be orphaned and removed from the game.

Add the following code to *board.js* after popBubbleAt:

```
var Board = function(){
  --snip--
  this.popBubbleAt = function(rowNum,colNum){
    --snip--
  };
  this.findOrphans = function(){
    var connected = [];
    var groups = [];
    var rows = that.getRows();
    for(var i=0;i<rows.length;i++){
      connected[i] = [];
    };
    for(var i=0;i<rows[0].length;i++){
      var bubble = that.getBubbleAt(0,i);
      if(bubble && !connected[0][i]){
        var group = that.getGroup(bubble,{},true);
        $.each(group.list,function(){
          connected[this.getRow()][this.getCol()] = true;
        });
      };
    };
    var orphaned = [];
    for(var i=0;i<rows.length;i++){
      for(var j=0;j<rows[i].length;j++){
        var bubble = that.getBubbleAt(i,j);
        if(bubble && !connected[i][j]){
          orphaned.push(bubble);
        };
      };
    };
    return orphaned;
  };
  return this;
};
```

Let's analyze the findOrphans function more closely. First, we set up the arrays we need to find orphaned groups.

```
❶ var connected = [];
❷ var groups = [];
  var rows = that.getRows();
  for(var i=0;i<rows.length;i++){
    connected[i] = [];
  };
```

The connected array ❶ is a two-dimensional array of rows and columns; it marks the locations of connected bubbles. The groups array ❷ will contain a set of all the groups found, which will be a single group if the entire board is connected. Next, we examine each bubble in the top row.

```
for(var i=0;i<rows[0].length;i++){
  var bubble = that.getBubbleAt(0,i);
```

Here, because we're only interested in bubbles connected to the top row, we loop over just the top row and fetch bubbles to check. When we have a bubble, we can start creating groups.

```
  if(bubble && !connected[0][i]){
    var group = that.getGroup(bubble,{},true);
```

If a bubble is present and this space hasn't already been marked as connected, we build a group. The call to getGroup passes true as the third parameter (differentColor), because we don't want to restrict connected bubbles by color.

```
    $.each(group.list,function(){
      connected[this.getRow()][this.getCol()] = true;
    });
  };
};
```

Because the bubble being checked is connected via the first row, the entire group is connected; therefore, we mark each entry in the connected array with a true flag.

After calling findOrphans, we should have an array of connected row and column entries. A list of orphaned bubbles is the final output we want, so we need to create another empty array to hold that list. A single-dimensional array is sufficient because the bubbles store their own coordinates:

```
var orphaned = [];
for(var i=0;i<rows.length;i++){
  for(var j=0;j<rows[i].length;j++){
    var bubble = that.getBubbleAt(i,j);
    if(bubble && !connected[i][j]){
      orphaned.push(bubble);
    };
  };
};
return orphaned;
};
```

Using this new array, we examine all the rows and columns on the board, checking whether a bubble exists at each space. If a bubble exists but no entry is in the connected grid, it's an orphan. We then add it to the orphaned list with the call to `orphaned.push(bubble)`. Finally, `findOrphans` returns the array of orphaned bubbles, which should be empty if no orphans exist.

Dropping Orphaned Bubbles

Now that we can find the groups of bubbles that will be orphaned, we need to call the function and remove any identified orphaned bubbles. Rather than pop, we want the orphaned bubbles to drop, using an animation that occurs after the popping animation has completed. The internal game state will still update instantaneously, because we calculate the outcome as soon as the player has fired the bubble. We add the delay not just to provide a more dramatic effect, but also so players can follow the results of their actions onscreen. If we animated the falling orphaned groups as soon as we knew they would be orphaned, the effect might be lost. In addition, players might be confused as to why bubbles of different colors had disappeared.

In this situation, the benefits of separating game state from display state are apparent. We update the game state instantly, players can fire their next bubble almost immediately without having to wait for completed animations, and the game feels responsive. But in the display state, we make a big deal of this game state change—for effect and to communicate how the player's actions lead to the final result. The animation approach is very much a game design decision rather than a coding one, but the way we've coded the game allows for flexibility.

In *game.js*, add the following after the call to `popBubbles`:

game.js

```
var Game = function(){
  --snip--
  var clickGameScreen = function(e){
    --snip--
    if(collision){
      --snip--
❶     if(group.list.length >= 3){
        popBubbles(group.list,duration);
❷       var orphans = board.findOrphans();
❸       var delay = duration + 200 + 30 * group.list.length;
❹       dropBubbles(orphans,delay);
      };
    }else{
      --snip--
    };
    BubbleShoot.ui.fireBubble(curBubble,coords,duration);
    curBubble = getNextBubble();
  };
};
```

We need to check for new orphans only if bubbles have been popped ❶, because that's how orphaned groups are formed. We pop bubbles only if a matching group of three or more is created, so if `group.list` is greater than or equal to three, we need to look for orphaned bubbles. As we retrieve the orphans ❷, we calculate a delay ❸ timed to drop bubbles when all the popping has finished. To perform the animation, we need to write dropBubbles ❹.

The dropBubbles method will drop the bubbles off the screen. Add the following code after the close of the popBubbles function in *game.js*:

game.js

```
var Game = function(){
  --snip--
  var popBubbles = function(bubbles,delay){
    --snip--
  };
  var dropBubbles = function(❶bubbles,delay){
    $.each(bubbles,function(){
      var bubble = this;
❷    board.popBubbleAt(bubble.getRow(),bubble.getCol());
      setTimeout(function(){
❸      bubble.getSprite().animate({
          top : 1000
        },1000);
      },delay);
    });
  };
};
```

The dropBubbles function takes in parameters for the bubbles to drop ❶ (we'll pass it the array of bubbles returned by findOrphans) and a delay. It removes the bubbles from the board ❷ and then animates them as they drop down the screen ❸.

Refresh the game and pop a few groups of bubbles. When you form an orphan group, the bubbles should drop off the screen rather than popping.

Exploding Bubbles with a jQuery Plug-in

Although dropping bubbles is an animation, it's not very dramatic. Let's liven it up and create more of an explosion! We'll write a jQuery plug-in to control this animation and abstract it from the game system.

To make the orphaned bubbles animation more impressive, we'll make the bubbles burst outward before dropping down the screen. We'll do this by assigning a starting momentum to each bubble and then adjusting its speed with some simulated gravity.

Although writing all the code to do this inline inside dropBubbles is possible, it would start to clutter the Game class with display logic. However, this animation is an ideal candidate for a jQuery plug-in, and the advantage is that we can reuse the code in future projects.

NOTE *For this example, I'll cover only the most basic principles of writing jQuery plug-ins. You can explore plug-ins in more depth at* http://learn.jquery.com/plugins/basic-plugin-creation/.

Make a new file called *jquery.kaboom.js* in the *_js* folder and add it to the `Modernizr.load` call. The file-naming convention informs others glancing in your *scripts* folder that this file is a jQuery plug-in; they don't even need to look at the code.

First, we register the method—which we'll name `kaboom`—by using jQuery's plug-in format:

jquery .kaboom.js

```
(function(jQuery){
  jQuery.fn.kaboom = function(settings)
  {
  };
})(jQuery);
```

We'll flesh out this code shortly; right now it doesn't do anything. This function definition is the standard way of registering a new plug-in with jQuery. Its structure enables calls of the form `$(...).kaboom()`, including passing an optional settings parameter.

The call to `kaboom` will be inside `dropBubbles`, so let's add that call to `dropBubbles` and remove the animate calls:

game.js

```
var Game = function(){
  --snip--
  var popBubbles = function(bubbles,delay){
    --snip--
  };
  var dropBubbles = function(bubbles,delay){
    $.each(bubbles,function(){
      var bubble = this;
      board.popBubbleAt(bubble.getRow(),bubble.getCol());
      setTimeout(function(){
        bubble.getSprite().kaboom();
      },delay);
    });
    return;
  };
};
```

The `kaboom` method will be called once for each object. This method will also only operate on jQuery objects; as a jQuery plug-in, it will have no knowledge of the game objects and will work only with DOM elements, making the plug-in reusable in future games.

Inside `jquery.fn.kaboom`, we'll use an array to store all the objects currently being exploded. Every time we call `kaboom`, we'll add the calling object to that array. When the bubble has finished moving, it should remove itself from the list. By storing everything we want to move in an array, we can run a single `setTimeout` loop and update the position of all falling bubbles at the same time. Consequently, we'll avoid having multiple `setTimeouts` clamoring for processing power, and the animation should run much more smoothly.

We'll also add two more components: some default parameters for gravity and the distance we want a bubble to fall before we consider it off the screen and no longer part of the function.

jquery .kaboom.js

```
(function(jQuery){
❶   var defaults = {
      gravity : 1.3,
      maxY : 800
    };
❷   var toMove = [];
    jQuery.fn.kaboom = function(settings){
    }
})(jQuery);
```

The default values are gravity and maxY ❶, and toMove ❷ will hold the falling jQuery objects.

At present, nothing happens when kaboom is called. The full jquery.kaboom plug-in follows:

jquery .kaboom.js

```
(function(jQuery){
    var defaults = {
      gravity : 1.3,
      maxY : 800
    };
    var toMove = [];
❶   jQuery.fn.kaboom = function(settings){
      var config = $.extend({}, defaults, settings);
      if(toMove.length == 0){
        setTimeout(moveAll,40);
      };
      var dx = Math.round(Math.random() * 10) - 5;
      var dy = Math.round(Math.random() * 5) + 5;
      toMove.push({
        elm : this,
        dx : dx,
        dy : dy,
        x : this.position().left,
        y : this.position().top,
        config : config
      });
    };
❷   var moveAll = function(){
      var frameProportion = 1;
      var stillToMove = [];
      for(var i=0;i<toMove.length;i++){
        var obj = toMove[i];
        obj.x += obj.dx * frameProportion;
        obj.y -= obj.dy * frameProportion;
        obj.dy -= obj.config.gravity * frameProportion;
        if(obj.y < obj.config.maxY){
```

```
            obj.elm.css({
              top : Math.round(obj.y),
              left : Math.round(obj.x)
            });
            stillToMove.push(obj);
          }else if(obj.config.callback){
              obj.config.callback();
      }
    };
    toMove = stillToMove;
    if(toMove.length > 0)
        setTimeout(moveAll,40);
    };
})(jQuery);
```

Two main loops are in this plug-in: jQuery.fn.kaboom ❶, which adds new elements to the animation queue, and moveAll ❷, which handles the animation.

Let's look at jQuery.fn.kaboom in more detail first:

```
  jQuery.fn.kaboom = function(settings){
❶   var config = $.extend({}, defaults, settings);
❷   if(toMove.length == 0){
      setTimeout(moveAll,40);
    };
❸   var dx = Math.round(Math.random() * 10) - 5;
    var dy = Math.round(Math.random() * 5) + 5;
❹   toMove.push({
      elm : $(this),
      dx : dx,
      dy : dy,
      x : $(this).position().left,
      y : $(this).position().top,
      config : config
    });
  };
```

This function initiates the animation process and is only called once per object (that is, it doesn't run as part of an animation loop). The function then sets the config options ❶ for this call to kaboom. The syntax creates an object with defaults set in the parent definition (the defaults variable) and overrides these settings with any found in the object that's been passed. It also adds any new name/value pairs to the object kaboom will act on.

We look in the array toMove and, if the array is empty ❷, set a timeout call that runs the animation. Next, values for the initial x and y velocities are set in dx and dy ❸. These values are between –5 and 5 pixels horizontally and between 5 and 10 pixels vertically (upward); both have units of pixels per second. We then add a new object to the toMove array ❹. The new object contains the jQuery element, its newly created velocity information, the current screen position, and the config options that were specified within this call.

The jQuery.fn.kaboom function runs whenever a $(...).kaboom call is made. If at least one object is exploding, a timeout containing moveAll will be running. Let's look at what the moveAll function does:

```
var moveAll = function(){
❶  var frameProportion = 1;
❷  var stillToMove = [];
❸  for(var i=0;i<toMove.length;i++){
      var obj = toMove[i];
❹    obj.x += obj.dx * frameProportion;
      obj.y -= obj.dy * frameProportion;
❺    obj.dy -= obj.config.gravity * frameProportion;
❻    if(obj.y < obj.config.maxY){
        obj.elm.css({
          top : Math.round(obj.y),
          left : Math.round(obj.x)
        });
        stillToMove.push(obj);
❼    }else if(obj.config.callback){
        obj.config.callback();
      }
    };
❽  toMove = stillToMove;
    if(toMove.length > 0)
❾    setTimeout(moveAll,40);
};
```

We assume that setTimeout is indeed running every 40 milliseconds because it's the value we specify ❾; therefore, we count the frame rate as 25 per second ❶. If a computer is underpowered (or just busy using CPU cycles on another operation) and the delay between frames is much slower than 40 milliseconds, this assumption may result in a poor animation quality. Later, you'll learn how to produce an animation at constant speed regardless of processor power, but the current solution provides the best compatibility in legacy browsers.

After setting the frame rate, moveAll creates an empty array ❷ to store any objects that don't move past the maximum value of *y* by the end of the animation frame. The resulting value here will become the new value for toMove to move again on the next frame.

With the setup work done, moveAll loops ❸ over each element in the toMove array (that is, all the objects currently in the state of exploding; we populated this array in jQuery.fn.kaboom) and grabs a reference to each one in the obj variable, which is an object with the following properties:

- obj.elm pointing to the jQuery object
- dx and dy velocity values
- *x*- and *y*-coordinates storing the current position

Inside the loop, we change the x and y values ❹ by a proportion of the object's x and y velocities, respectively. This doesn't affect the bubble's screen position yet because we haven't manipulated the DOM element. The function also adds the configured gravity setting to the object's vertical velocity ❺. Horizontal velocity should remain constant throughout the explosion effect, but the object will accelerate downward to simulate falling. Next, we check ❻ to see if the object has a value of y that exceeds the maximum we either configured in defaults or overrode in the call to kaboom. If it doesn't, the position of the screen element is set to the values stored for the current position, and we add the object to the stillToMove array. On the other hand, if the object *has* passed the maximum y and a callback function was passed as part of the original kaboom call, moveAll runs ❼ that function. It's useful to pass a function into an animation and have that function run when the animation is complete.

Finally, we set the new value of toMove ❽ to be the contents of stillToMove (that is, all the objects that are still falling), and if the array contains at least one element, we set a timeout to call the same function again in another 40 milliseconds ❾.

Now, when you reload the game and create an orphaned group of objects, the kaboom plug-in should make bubbles drop down the screen. Although it works within our game context, you could call it with any valid jQuery selector and produce a similar result. Keep the code handy so you can reuse the effect in future games!

Summary

Quite a bit of *Bubble Shooter* is in place now. We can fire bubbles that either settle into the grid or pop groups, and we can detect orphaned groups and drop them off the screen. However, the board can get clogged with unpopped bubbles, and that's a problem we still need to solve. Currently, there's also no way to start another level or keep track of your score; both are important elements for this type of game. But before we complete some of the other game functionality, we'll dive into some HTML5 and CSS implementations of the animations we've already written.

So far, we've achieved the features needed with some fairly traditional HTML, CSS, and JavaScript techniques. For the most part, the game should run smoothly on most computers. In the next chapter, we'll improve performance by offloading some of the animation work from JavaScript to CSS. The shift will let us take advantage of hardware acceleration when possible, and we'll even use some pure HTML5 features for smoother animation. We'll also implement the entire game using canvas rendering rather than DOM and CSS, revealing the advantages and the challenges that result using that approach.

Further Practice

1. In the exercises in Chapter 3, you changed createLayout to generate alternative grid patterns. Test your layouts now with the popping and orphan-dropping code. Does the code work? How do your patterns affect the feel of the game?

2. Bubble animations currently consist of four frames. Create your own versions of the images and try adding more frames. Use a for loop to generate the extra setTimeout calls rather than copying and pasting new lines. Experiment with the timeout delays to speed up and slow down the animation and see which values produce the best effect.

3. The kaboom jQuery plug-in drops the bubbles off the bottom of the screen, but what would happen if you made the bubbles bounce when they hit the bottom? Amend *jquery.kaboom.js* so the bubbles bounce instead of drop off the screen. You'll need to reverse their dy values and scale them down each time they bounce to mimic some of the bounce energy being absorbed; otherwise, they'll just bounce back to the same height. The bubbles should be removed from the DOM only when they've bounced off either the left or the right edge of the screen, so you'll also need to ensure that the value of dx isn't close to zero, or they'll never disappear.

PART 2

ENHANCEMENTS WITH
HTML5 AND THE CANVAS

5

CSS TRANSITIONS AND TRANSFORMATIONS

 So far, we've created a bare-bones game with HTML, CSS, and JavaScript: we can fire and pop bubbles, and our user interface feels responsive. We achieved this through Document Object Model (DOM) manipulation with a lot of jQuery help.

In this chapter, we'll explore CSS transitions and transformations, which can improve game performance and let you create a wider range of effects, such as rotating and scaling elements.

Benefits of CSS

CSS provides a set of transformation and transition attributes that you can use to animate changes to CSS properties, such as the left or top coordinates of an element. Rather than using JavaScript to handle animations frame by frame, as we've done so far, CSS transitions are specified in the style sheet or as styles attached to DOM elements. An animation is then initiated by making a single change to a CSS property rather than making many incremental changes to a property, as JavaScript animations require.

CSS animations are handled by the browser's rendering engine rather than by the JavaScript interpreter, freeing up CPU time for running other JavaScript code and ensuring the smoothest animation possible on the device at the time. On systems with graphics processors, the effects are often handled entirely by the graphics processor, which means less work for the JavaScript code you are running and can reduce the load on the CPU even further, resulting in higher frame rates. As a result, the animation will run at the highest frame rate possible for the device it's displayed on.

We'll use CSS to add some simple transitions to user-interface elements and then replace our jQuery animations with transformations, and we'll do this while maintaining the cross-browser compatibility that we've achieved thus far.

Basic CSS Transitions

The first CSS animation we'll focus on is the transition. A *transition* defines how a style property of an object should change from one state to a new one. For example, if we change the `left` property of a DOM element from 50 pixels to 500 pixels, it will instantly change position on the screen. But if we specify a transition, we can instead make it move gradually across the screen. A CSS transition specifies a property or properties to animate, how the animation should take place, and how long the animation should take.

Transitions generally apply to any CSS property that has a numerical value. For example, animating the `left` property, as mentioned earlier, is possible because intermediate values between the beginning and end can be calculated. Other property changes, such as between `visibility : hidden` and `visibility : visible`, are not valid properties for a transition because intermediate values cannot be calculated. However, we could make an element fade in by animating the `opacity` property from 0 to 1.

Colors are also valid properties to animate, because hex values are also numbers (each contains three pairs, and each pair represents red, green, or blue) that can be gradually changed from one value to another. You can find a list of all the properties that can be animated with transitions at *https://developer.mozilla.org/en-US/docs/Web/CSS/CSS_animated_properties/*.

How to Write a Transition

To animate a `div` using a transition, add a CSS transition property to it. A transition property includes the following:

CSS properties to apply the transition to   These can be any valid CSS properties that you want to animate, such as `top`, `left`, `font-size`, or just `all`, which applies transitions to all valid property changes.

Duration   How long (in seconds) the transition will take.

Easing Tells a property how fast to change over the transition duration. For example, an element might move from one point to another at a smooth pace, or it could accelerate at the beginning and then decelerate toward the end, as in Figure 5-1. You can apply easing to other properties you want to change, too, including color.

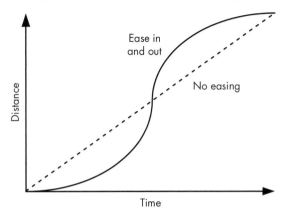

Figure 5-1: Graph showing movement with no easing and movement with easing in (at the start of the animation) and out (at the end).

Start delay Specifies the number of seconds to wait to start the transition. The most common value is 0 (or empty), which means start immediately.

We'll write a transition definition just like any other CSS rule, and when we want the transition to occur, we'll make a change to the CSS property that we want to animate. To move a div or other HTML element smoothly across the screen, we set the top and left coordinates to new values:

```
transition: top 1s, left 2s (etc)
```

As an example, we'll make the New Game button move down the screen. Add the following to *main.css*:

main.css
```
.button
{
  transition: ❶all ❷.8s ❸ease-in-out ❹1s;
❺ -moz-transition: all .8s ease-in-out 1s;
  -webkit-transition: all .8s ease-in-out 1s;
  -ms-transition: all .8s ease-in-out 1s;
}
```

The transition definition's first value ❶ states which property (or properties) the transition applies to. Using all applies the transition to every property; think of it as a wildcard. The second value ❷ is the duration of the transition in seconds. The third value ❸ is the easing: ease-in-out produces a smooth transition with an initial acceleration and ending deceleration. Finally, we add a delay ❹ of 1 second before the animation runs. The next three lines beginning at ❺ provide the same specification but with vendor-specific prefixes for cross-browser support. These are needed for older browsers; newer browsers use the unprefixed version once the tag definition is considered to be stable.

To guarantee your game will run on a certain browser, always include the correct vendor-specific prefix. Just be sure that whenever you change a transition's property, you also change it in the transition definition for each browser.

Fortunately, the rule is simple: the browser-specific versions of transition are just copies of the regular version with one of the following prefixes:

- -moz- for Mozilla browsers, such as Firefox
- -webkit- for Webkit browsers, such as Chrome and Safari
- -ms- for Microsoft Internet Explorer

Reload the page and then type the following into the JavaScript console:

```
$(".but_start_game").css("top",100)
```

You should see a pause, and then the button will smoothly slide up the screen. The effect is more or less identical to an animate call, but we changed only the CSS value.

Delete the CSS definition for .button now because we're going to apply a more useful effect.

Color-Changing Buttons

Let's apply transitions to spice up our user interface! We'll animate a button without a single line of JavaScript; instead, we'll use a transition definition and the hover pseudo-class that you're probably familiar with for creating rollover button effects.

First, we'll add a rollover state to the New Game button with a CSS amendment. Add the following to *main.css* now:

main.css

```
.button
{
  transition: ❶background-color ❷.3s ❸ease-in-out;
❹ -moz-transition: background-color .3s ease-in-out;
  -webkit-transition: background-color .3s ease-in-out;
  -ms-transition: background-color .3s ease-in-out;
}
  .button:hover
  {
    background-color: #900;
  }
```

The transition definition's first value ❶ states which property (or properties) the transition applies to. We're applying it to the background-color property, which is written exactly as it would appear as a standard CSS rule. The second value ❷ is the length of the transition in seconds. The third value ❸ is once again the easing, set to ease-in-out.

Other types of easing include ease, linear, or just ease-in or ease-out. But all of these shorthand descriptions are actually aliases for specific definitions of cubic-bezier, which you can use to indicate any transition curve you like. The cubic-bezier easing function accepts four decimal numbers to define a graph; for example,

```
transition: background-color .3s ease-in-out;
```

is identical to

```
transition: background-color .3s cubic-bezier(0.42, 0, 0.58, 1.0)
```

Bézier curves are described by specifying the coordinates of two points that form the tangent line of the beginning and the end parts of the curve, respectively. These are shown as P1 and P2 in Figure 5-2.

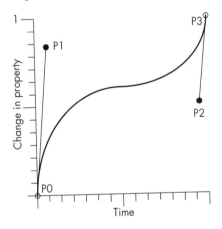

Figure 5-2: The two points that specify a Bézier curve are P1 and P2.

The values specified in the CSS are the coordinates of P1 and P2, which are always between 0 and 1. You won't specify P0 and P3 because they're always the origin (0,0) and (1,1), respectively. The angle of P1 and P2 from the vertical axis determines the slope of the curve, and the length of the lines from P0 to P1 and P2 to P3 determines how pronounced the curvature will be.

Unless you want a specific easing, ease-in-out or linear will often do just fine. But for more complex transitions, some online tools will help you create cubic-bezier curves based on visual graphs and input values. One such website is *http://cubic-bezier.com/*, which allows you to tweak values and watch the animation to see how the numbers translate to a movement transition.

The three lines, starting after the initial transition definition at ❹, are vendor-specific transition definitions, which I made sure to include so the transition works properly in different browsers. The CSS standard is still considered a work in progress, and browser manufacturers have adopted their own prefixes to avoid potential conflicts with how the standard is implemented when it's finalized.

The single-line format I've used so far is the most compact way to specify a transition, but you could also specify the properties individually:

```
transition-property: background-color;
transition-duration: .3s;
transition-timing-function: ease-in-out;
```

I recommend sticking with the compact approach most of the time. Otherwise, you'd need all the CSS standard lines plus the three vendor-specific copies of each, which would quickly clutter your style sheet.

Reload the page and hover over the New Game button. You should see a gentle change in color from light to darker red. That's a nice effect, and you didn't write any JavaScript! But there's still more you can do to add effects using CSS only.

Basic CSS Transformations

The second powerful feature of CSS we'll look at is transformations. *Transformations* allow you to manipulate an object's shape. In most browsers, it's possible to transform an object in either two dimensions or three and to skew, distort, and rotate it in any way that can be described by a three-dimensional matrix. You can animate transformations with transitions or let them stand alone; for example, to display a button at an angle, you might let the viewer watch it rotate, or you might just render the button askew.

How to Write a Transformation

Some simple CSS transformations include:

- Translations by (*x,y*) or even (*x,y,z*) coordinates in 3D
- Scaling by dimensions along the *x*-, *y*-, and *z*-axes
- Rotating in place by an angle along any of the *x*-, *y*-, or *z*-axes
- Skewing along the *x*- or *y*-axis
- Adding 3D perspective

You can transform by a 2D or even a 3D matrix. Transforming by a matrix involves some calculation of the math involved. If you want to explore it in more depth, some references are available online, such as *https://developer.mozilla.org/en-US/docs/Web/CSS/transform/*.

Scaling a Button

In this section, we'll make the New Game button a bit more dynamic by adding an enlarging effect on top of the current color change. Make the following addition to the `.button:hover` definition in *main.css*:

main.css

```
.button:hover
{
  background-color: #900;
❶ transform: scale(1.1);
  -moz-transform: scale(1.1);
  -webkit-transform: scale(1.1);
  -ms-transform: scale(1.1);
}
```

The entire transformation is primarily contained in one transform line ❶. The transformation is specified as scaling by a factor of 1.1—a size increase of 10 percent. The three lines that follow do the same thing but use the identical vendor-specific prefixes you used in the `transition` definition.

We just want to scale the New Game button, so reload the page and then mouse over the button again. The scaling should work but not as a smooth animation. Although the color still changes gradually in response to the mouse hover, the button's size jumps in a single step. We'll amend the transition definition to apply to the transform as well as the background color.

To achieve this task, we could simply change the `.button` definition so the transition property affects every CSS property:

```
transition: all .3s ease-in-out;
```

This definition applies the ease-in-out effect to all of the button's CSS properties that it's possible to apply transitions to. Now if any of those properties change after the DOM is rendered, the button will be animated with a 300-millisecond transition effect on that property. But what if you don't want all button animations to happen at the same rate?

In that case, you could specify multiple properties by adding a comma-separated definition:

```
transition: background-color .2s ease-in-out, transform 0.2s ease-in-out;
```

This solution also minimizes side effects if we want to change any other CSS properties on the fly without having them animate automatically.

When you apply transitions to individual `transform` properties in CSS, you still need to specify vendor-specific versions within each transition definition. Therefore, the full button definition needs to be this:

```
.button
{
  transition: background-color .3s ease-in-out, transform .2s ease-in-out;
  -moz-transition: background-color .3s ease-in-out, -moz-transform .2s
ease-in-out;
```

```
    -webkit-transition: background-color .3s ease-in-out, -webkit-transform .2s
ease-in-out;
    -ms-transition: background-color .3s ease-in-out, -ms-transform .2s ease-in-
out;
}
```

Make this change in *main.css*, reload the page, and mouse over the button again. Now, both the background color and scale should change in a smooth transition.

CSS transitions and transformations are useful for simple animations and especially for mouseover effects on user-interface elements, such as buttons. However, they're useful for more than just adding a bit of sparkle to the user interface: we can also use them to animate sprites, including the fired bubbles in the game.

CSS Transitions in Place of jQuery animate

Now, when a player fires a bubble, it leaves the firing point and moves in a straight line toward its destination. Any fired bubble follows a path simple enough that a CSS transition can handle that animation easily, and making the switch will remove some of the load from JavaScript.

The hard-coded CSS transition we used for the button hover effect, where the transition is defined in the style sheet, won't work for bubble movement because the duration of the transition needs to change depending on how far the bubble has to move. Currently, a bubble moves at 1,000 pixels per second. So for example, if we want a bubble to move 200 pixels, the duration needs to be set at 200 milliseconds. To handle this variable duration, instead of specifying the CSS transitions in the style sheet, we'll apply them at runtime with JavaScript.

Setting a CSS transition with jQuery uses the same syntax as setting any other CSS property, but we'll need to add browser prefixes for property names. Fortunately, we don't have to write four versions of the same transition for this task. Modernizr can take care of those prefixes for us, which actually makes it easier to create CSS transitions in JavaScript than in a style sheet!

However, not all older browsers support transitions, so inside *ui.js* we'll first check whether CSS animations are supported and fall back to the jQuery animation if they're not. Unless you're sure that CSS transitions are supported in all of the browsers you're targeting, it's a good idea to build in a fallback option.

The code for this CSS animation involves three steps:

1. Add the transition CSS property to the element to tell it how quickly to move and which property to apply the transition to.

2. Change the `top` and `left` properties to the coordinates we want the bubble to stop at.

3. Once the bubble has reached its destination, remove the CSS transition definition.

Amend `fireBubble` in *ui.js* as follows:

```
var BubbleShoot = window.BubbleShoot || {};
BubbleShoot.ui = (function($){
  var ui = {
    --snip--
    fireBubble : function(bubble,coords,duration){
❶      var complete = function(){
❷        if(bubble.getRow() !== null){
❸          bubble.getSprite().css(Modernizr.prefixed("transition"),"");
          bubble.getSprite().css({
            left : bubble.getCoords().left - ui.BUBBLE_DIMS/2,
            top : bubble.getCoords().top - ui.BUBBLE_DIMS/2
          });
        };
      };
❹      if(Modernizr.csstransitions){
❺        bubble.getSprite().css(Modernizr.prefixed("transition"),"all " +
          (duration/1000) + "s linear");
        bubble.getSprite().css({
          left : coords.x - ui.BUBBLE_DIMS/2,
          top : coords.y - ui.BUBBLE_DIMS/2
        });
❻        setTimeout(complete,duration);
      }else{
❼        bubble.getSprite().animate({
            left : coords.x - ui.BUBBLE_DIMS/2,
            top : coords.y - ui.BUBBLE_DIMS/2
          },
          {
            duration : duration,
            easing : "linear",
            complete : complete
          });
      }
    },
    --snip--
  };
  return ui;
} )(jQuery);
```

We've moved the post-animation function—the one we want jQuery to call once the animate call has been completed—into its own named definition ❶ by assigning it to a variable. This function ensures that if the bubble hasn't disappeared off the screen, it's finally positioned within the board grid. This function is identical to the previous version in that first we check to see whether the bubble has a row definition ❷. If the row definition is null, the bubble missed the board or caused a popping event. Otherwise, the bubble needs to become part of the main board. In that case, we also remove ❸ the transition definition and move the bubble to its final position. Consequently, if we apply any CSS changes to the bubble in the future, an unwanted transition won't be applied to them.

When `fireBubble` is called, we check that CSS transitions are supported using Modernizr ❹. If they are supported, we can add the transition CSS to the bubble element ❺. The transition definition will take the form

```
transform: all [duration]s linear
```

`Modernizr.prefixed("transition")` adds any necessary vendor-specific prefixes. We set the transition duration to be the same as the duration passed in but divide it by a thousand to convert from milliseconds to seconds ❺.

Finally, if we did add a transition, we set a timeout ❻ to call `complete` when that transition ends. We don't need the `setTimeout` call if a browser doesn't support CSS because, in that case, we'll use the jQuery `animate` function, which accepts a callback function to run once an animation completes. We need to add the `complete` function as a parameter to that `animate` call ❼, but essentially, the jQuery version of the animation is the same as before.

Refresh the page, fire a bubble, and most likely you'll see no change in the game from the last time you tested it. But that just means your device could display the jQuery animation we asked it to before at a high enough frame rate that it's indistinguishable from the CSS version. Behind the scenes, that animation is now being passed off to the graphics processor, if your device has one, so JavaScript doesn't have to handle the processing load. In games with numerous moving elements, the change you just made could result in a noticeable performance increase.

Disadvantages of CSS Transitions

If JavaScript has to do so much work to animate an element frame by frame, why not use CSS transitions wherever possible? Although CSS transitions offer a number of benefits, particularly when it comes to smooth animations, their usefulness in games is often limited by a lack of control.

CSS transitions become more cumbersome to compose as you add more animations to a single element. For example, if you want an element to move by 100 pixels over a duration of 1 second and you also resize it by 10 pixels over 2 seconds, you need to specify a different transition for each CSS property. More important, at the end of the movement transition, you'll need to retain the CSS definition so the resize animation continues, which is especially difficult if you need to move the element again.

A second disadvantage of transitions is that although easing can alter the way an animation appears, movement must be in a straight line. Movement along a curve, as in an animation of a character jumping over something, could be generated by animating over many small straight line segments. But in that case, you may as well use JavaScript for the entire animation.

Once set in motion, CSS transitions are impossible to interrogate and change. The browser handles the transition and updates the element's position as soon as you set the value in CSS. The element may be rendered halfway to its destination due to the transition, but the DOM will report that it's already done moving. As a result, it is impossible to interrogate an element for its current position until the animation ends. If you wanted to apply a change in direction, you'd need to perform new calculations and rewrite your CSS transition.

For example, if you tell an element to change its left position from 50 pixels to 250 pixels over 2 seconds, but after 1 second you need to move it to a different screen position, you would first need to calculate where it sits on the screen after 1 second. The DOM would report its left position at 250 pixels, but we know that it's at the midpoint of an animation, which would put it at 150 pixels in *most* cases. But if you had specified easing along a cubic Bézier curve, the element is unlikely to be at the midpoint and indeed may be quite far from it. You would need to write an equation to calculate the current left coordinate. This example is simpler than most because we stop the element midway, but with any kind of easing applied and at almost any other point along the animation path, calculating where an element might be drawn on the screen is no simple task.

Compare this example to animating with jQuery, in which you can just call the .stop method after 1,000 milliseconds to stop an element dead in its tracks. With jQuery, you can even apply a new animate method to set a sprite on an entirely new path without waiting for a previous animation to finish. CSS transformations and transitions work well for user-interface manipulation or for relatively simple straight-line movement, but they don't provide the flexibility we need for a lot of in-game action.

Summary

You've seen how simple and powerful CSS transitions can be, but also how their usefulness can be limited for in-game action. You've also taken a brief look at CSS transformations that can be used in combination with transitions to add special effects to buttons or other HTML elements.

One of the main advantages of CSS transitions over JavaScript animation is their rendering speed, but unfortunately they are not easy to work with for anything other than the simplest of animations. In the next chapter, we'll look at the canvas element and see how we can animate games with greater speed and control than DOM-based development has given us.

Further Practice

1. Using the CSS transition example in which we animated the New Game button, experiment with some Bézier curve easing. Think about how different values might be useful in game animations.

2. Create a transformation matrix to flip an element from left to right to make it appear mirrored.

3. Common 2D CSS transformations include translate, rotate, scale, and skew. Which of these can you reproduce using a matrix transformation, and which can't you reproduce?

6

RENDERING CANVAS SPRITES

 Up until now, we've built *Bubble Shooter* with a DOM-based approach by using HTML elements for game objects that are styled and positioned by CSS and manipulated by JavaScript. In this chapter, we'll rework *Bubble Shooter* so most of the game area is rendered to a canvas instead of using the DOM. Our game's dialogs will remain in HTML and CSS.

Canvas rendering allows us to achieve graphical effects that are often impossible with DOM-based development, and it can often provide a faster rendering speed. To use canvas rendering for *Bubble Shooter*, we need to learn how to render entire scenes to the canvas, maintain state, and perform frame-by-frame animations.

We'll keep the existing DOM-rendering code in place for devices where the canvas element isn't supported and provide progressive enhancement to the canvas for more modern browsers. We'll do this to demonstrate the principle involved in coding for both canvas- and DOM-based animation and to highlight the differences between the two approaches.

Detecting Canvas Support

Modernizr can help us detect canvas features so we don't have to remember multiple cross-browser cases. We'll load in only a couple of extra JavaScript files for the canvas version and won't delete any files. To detect the canvas and load in the right files, we need an extra node in Modernizr.load in *index.html*, which will check for canvas support, and if present, load JavaScript files from an array. Add the following before *game.js* is loaded:

index.html

```
},
{
  test: Modernizr.canvas,
  yep: ["_js/renderer.js","_js/sprite.js"]
},
{
  load: "_js/game.js",
  complete: function(){
    $(function(){
      var game = new BubbleShoot.Game();
      game.init();
    })
  }
}]);
```

The value of Modernizr.canvas, the parameter that test looks for, will be either true or false. If it's true, the two files listed in yep are loaded; if it's false, nothing new happens.

Create empty files for *renderer.js* and *sprite.js* in the *_js* folder. The Renderer object will draw the game state at each frame, and the Sprite class will perform many of the operations that we've been using jQuery for to date. We want Renderer to be responsible for drawing pixels onto the canvas and not mix up game logic with it; likewise, we'll try to keep state information inside the relevant objects. This approach makes it much easier to switch between rendering using the canvas or the DOM, depending on what we think is best for the game.

Drawing to the Canvas

With HTML5's canvas feature, you can build games at a level of sophistication similar to that of Flash games or even native applications. You place canvas elements into documents in the same way as other elements, such as <div> or <img>, but it's the way you work with the element that makes it

Contra Costa County Library
Concord
8/30/2019 4:52:57 PM

- Patron Receipt -
- Charges -

ID.   21901024705067

Item 31901056136239
Title: Build an HTML5 game : a developer's
Call Number: 794 81526 BUNYAN 2015
Due Date: 9/20/2019

All Contra Costa County Libraries will be
closed on Sunday, Sept 1st, Monday, Sept 2
and Monday, October 14th. Items may be
renewed at ccclib.org or by calling
1-800-984-4636, menu option 1. Book drops
will be open. El Sobrante Library remains
closed for repairs.

different. Inside the canvas, you have pixel-level control, and you can draw to individual pixels, read their values, and manipulate them. You can write JavaScript code to generate arcade shooters or even 3D games that are difficult to reproduce with a DOM-based approach.

THE DOM VS. THE CANVAS

HTML is primarily an information format; CSS was introduced as a way to format that information. Creating games using both technologies is really a misappropriation, and games like *Bubble Shooter* are feasible largely because browser vendors have made an effort to increase performance. Many of the processes that are invaluable in laying out documents, such as ensuring that text areas don't overlap or that text wraps around images, are practices that we don't need for laying out games. As game developers, we take on responsibility for ensuring the screen is laid out well, but, unfortunately for us, the browser still runs through all of these checks in the background.

For example, adding or removing elements in the DOM can be a relatively expensive operation in terms of processing power. The reason is that if we add or remove something, the browser needs to inspect it to ensure that the change doesn't have a domino effect on the rest of the document flow. If we were working with, say, an expanding menu on a website, we might want the browser to push a navigation area down if we add more elements to it. However, in a game it's more likely that we will be using position: absolute, and we definitely don't want the addition or removal of a new element to force everything surrounding it to be repositioned.

By contrast, when the browser sees a canvas element, it sees just an image. If we change the contents of the canvas, only the contents change. The browser doesn't need to consider whether this change will have a knock-on effect on the rest of the document.

Unlike CSS and HTML, the canvas doesn't let you rely on the browser to keep track of the positions of objects on the screen. Nothing automatically deals with layering or rendering backgrounds when a sprite moves over them because the canvas outputs a flat image for the browser to display. If sprite animation and movement with CSS is like moving papers around on a notice wall, canvas animation is more like working with a whiteboard: if you want to change something or move it, you'll have to erase an area and redraw it.

Canvas rendering also differs from CSS layout in that positioning of elements can't be offloaded to the browser. For example, with our existing DOM-based system, we can use a CSS transition to move the bubble visually from its firing position to wherever we want it to end up in the board layout. To do this takes only a couple of lines of code.

Canvas rendering, on the other hand, requires us to animate frame by frame in a way similar to the internal workings of jQuery. We must calculate how far a bubble is along its path and draw it at that position each time a frame update occurs.

On its own, animating on the canvas using JavaScript would be no more arduous than JavaScript animation using the DOM without jQuery or CSS transitions to fall back on, but the process is made more complex by the fact that if we want to change the contents of the canvas, we need to delete pixels and redraw them. Ways to optimize the redrawing process are available, but a basic approach is to draw the entire canvas afresh for each animation frame. This means that, if we want to move an object across the canvas, we have to render not just the object that we want to move but possibly every object in the scene.

We'll draw the game board and the current bubble using the canvas, but some components, such as dialogs, are better left as DOM elements. User interface components are generally easier to update as DOM elements, and the browser usually renders text more precisely with HTML than it would render text within a canvas element.

Now that we've decided to render the game with a canvas system, let's look at what that will involve. The key tasks are rendering the images and maintaining states for each bubble so that we know which bubbles are stationary, which are moving, and which are in the various stages of being popped.

Image Rendering

Any image you want to draw to the canvas must be preloaded so it's available to be drawn; otherwise, nothing appears. To do this, we'll create an in-memory Image object in JavaScript, set the image source to the sprite sheet, and attach an onload event handler to it so we know when it's finished loading. Currently, the game is playable once the init function in *game.js* has run and the New Game button has the startGame function attached to its click event:

```
$(".but_start_game").bind("click",startGame);
```

We still want this to happen, but we don't want it to happen until after the sprite sheet image has loaded. This will be the first task we'll tackle.

canvas Elements

Next, we need to know how to draw images onto the canvas. A canvas element is an HTML element just like any other: it can be inserted into the DOM, can have CSS styling applied, and behaves in much the same way as an image. For example, to create a canvas element, we add the following to *index.html*:

```
<canvas id="game_canvas " width="1000" height="620"></canvas>
```

This creates a canvas element with the dimensions of 1000 pixels wide by 620 pixels high. These dimensions are important because they establish the number of pixels that make up the canvas. However, we should also set these dimensions in CSS to establish the size of the canvas as it will appear on the page:

```
#game_canvas
{
  width: 1000px;
  height: 620px;
}
```

In the same way that an image can be rendered at scale, the canvas element can also be scaled. By setting the CSS dimensions to the same values as the HTML attributes, we ensure that we're drawing the canvas at a scale of 1:1. If we omitted the CSS, the canvas would be rendered at the width and height specified in the attributes, but it's good practice to specify layout dimensions within the style sheet. Not only does it help with code readability, but it also ensures that if the internal dimensions of the canvas are changed, the page layout won't break.

To draw an image onto the canvas using JavaScript, we first need to get a *context*, the object that you use to manipulate canvas contents, using the method getContext. A context tells the browser whether we're working in two dimensions or three. You would write something like this to indicate you want to work in two-dimensional space rather than three-dimensional space:

```
document.getElementById("game_canvas").getContext("2d");
```

Or to write this using jQuery:

```
$("#game_canvas").get(0).getContext("2d");
```

Note that the context is a property of the DOM node, not the jQuery object, because we're retrieving the first object in jQuery's set with the get(0) call. We need the DOM node because the basic jQuery library doesn't contain any special functions for working with canvas elements.

Now, to draw the image onto the canvas, we use the drawImage method of the context object:

```
document.getElementById("game_canvas").getContext("2d").
drawImage(imageObject,x,y);
```

Or again, to write this using jQuery:

```
$("#game_canvas").get(0).getContext("2d").drawImage(imageObject,x,y);
```

The parameters passed into `drawImage` are the `Image` object and then *x*- and *y*-coordinates at which to draw the image. These are pixels relative to the canvas context origin. By default, (0,0) is the top-left corner of the canvas.

We can also clear pixels from the canvas with the `clearRect` method:

```
$("#game_canvas").get(0).getContext("2d").clearRect(0, 0, 1000, 620);
```

The `clearRect` command removes all canvas pixels from the top-left corner (first two parameters) down to the bottom-right corner (last two parameters). Although you can just clear the canvas rectangle that you want to change, it's usually easier to clear the entire canvas and redraw it each frame. Again, the coordinates are relative to the context origin.

The context maintains a number of state properties about the canvas, such as the current line thickness, line colors, and font properties. Most important for drawing sprites, it also maintains the coordinates of the context origin and a rotation angle. In fact, you can draw an image at a set position on the canvas in two ways:

- Pass *x*- and *y*-coordinates into the `drawImage` function.
- Move the context origin and draw the image at the origin.

In practice, you'll see the same results with either method, but there is a reason it's often best to move—or *translate*—the context origin. If you want to draw an image onto the canvas at an angle, it's not the image that's rotated but the canvas context that's rotated prior to drawing the image.

Rotating the Canvas

The canvas is always rotated around its origin. If you want to rotate an image around its own center, first translate the canvas origin to a new origin at the center of the image. Then rotate the canvas by the angle at which you want to rotate the image *but in the opposite direction to the rotation you wanted to apply to the object.* Then draw the image as usual, rotate the canvas back to zero degrees around its new origin, and finally translate the canvas back to its initial origin. Figure 6-1 shows how this works.

For example, to draw an image that's 100 pixels across at coordinates (100,100) and rotate it by 30 degrees around its center, you could write the following:

```
❶ var canvas = $("#game_canvas").get(0);
❷ var context = canvas.getContext("2d");
❸ context.clearRect(0, 0, canvas.width, canvas.height);
❹ context.translate(150, 150);
❺ context.rotate(Math.PI/6);
❻ context.drawImage(imageObject, -50, -50);
❼ context.rotate(-Math.PI/6);
❽ context.translate(-150, -150);
```

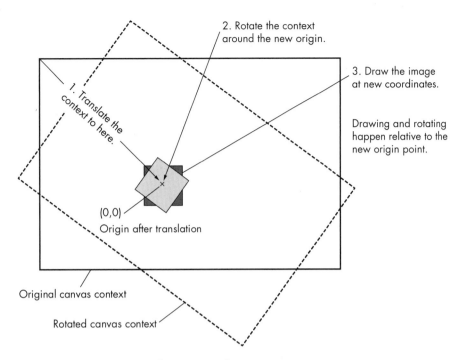

2. Rotate the context around the new origin.

3. Draw the image at new coordinates.

Drawing and rotating happen relative to the new origin point.

1. Translate the context to here.

(0,0)

Origin after translation

Original canvas context

Rotated canvas context

Figure 6-1: Drawing a rotated image onto the canvas

This code retrieves the canvas ❶ and the context ❷ and then clears the canvas so it's ready for drawing ❸. We next translate the origin to the coordinates at which we want to draw the image ❹, but we also need to add half the image's width and half of its height to the translation values, because we'll be drawing the center of the image at the new origin.

The next step is to add rotation ❺, but remember that we rotate the *context*, not the image. Angles are also specified in radians rather than degrees. The image is drawn at (-50,-50) ❻, which means that the center of the image is drawn at the context origin and then the context is rotated back ❼ and then translated back ❽. The last two steps are important because the context maintains state, so the next operation that's performed on the canvas would be on the rotated coordinates. By reversing the rotation and the translation, we have left the canvas in the same state in which we found it.

If you don't want to have to remember to rotate and translate the canvas back to its origin, you can simplify the whole process by storing the context before changing your image and resetting the context afterward:

```
var canvas = $("#game_canvas").get(0);
var context = canvas.getContext("2d");
context.clearRect(0, 0, canvas.width, canvas.height);
❶ context.save();
context.translate(150, 150);
context.rotate(Math.PI/6);
context.drawImage(imageObject, -50, -50);
❷ context.restore();
```

The call to `context.save` ❶ saves the current state of the context, although, importantly, it doesn't save the pixel data inside the canvas. Then `context.restore` ❷ sets it back to this saved state.

These principles are all we need to draw whole images onto the canvas and to remove them again, but to draw bubbles, we'll need to draw only a small section of the sprite sheet at a time.

CANVAS WIDTH AND HEIGHT

The canvas has its own settings for width and height, and it's important to specify these when you create a canvas element. You could use CSS to determine the dimensions of the canvas as displayed on the screen, but they may not match the number of pixels that the canvas internally is set to render. In our case, we'll make both the same, so drawing one pixel to the canvas will result in one pixel being displayed.

If we were to set the width and height of the canvas element to double what they are now, the DOM element would still take up the same amount of space on the page because of our CSS definition. The canvas interacts with CSS in the same way images do: the width and height are specified in the style sheet, but the canvas (or image) may be larger or smaller. The result is that the image we draw occupies only the top quarter of the canvas and appears to be a quarter of its original size. This happens because canvas pixels are scaled to screen pixels at render time. Try changing the canvas definition in *index.html* to the following and see what happens:

```
<canvas id="game_canvas" width="2000" height="1240"></canvas>
```

The canvas element won't appear any bigger on the screen because of the CSS rules. Instead, every pixel defined by CSS will be represented by 4 pixels on the canvas. In most desktop browsers, 1 CSS pixel is identical to 1 screen pixel, so there's little benefit to setting the canvas dimensions to values larger than those in the CSS. However, modern devices, especially mobile ones, have become sophisticated in their rendering and have what is called a higher pixel density. This allows the device to render much-higher-resolution images. You can read more about pixel density at *http://www.html5rocks.com/en/tutorials/canvas/hidpi/*.

When you're working with the canvas and CSS together, you need to remember which scale you're working at. If you're working within the canvas, it's the dimensions of the canvas, as specified by its HTML attributes, that are important. When working with CSS elements around—or possibly even on top of—the canvas, you'll be using CSS pixel dimensions. For example, to draw an image at the bottom-right of a canvas that is 2000 pixels wide and 1240 pixels high, you would use something like this:

```
$("#game_canvas").get(0).getContext("2d").drawImage(imageObject,2000,1240);
```

But to place a DOM element at the bottom-right corner, you would use the coordinates (1000,620), such as in the following CSS:

```
{
  left: 1000px;
  top: 620px;
}
```

If possible, it's generally easiest to keep your screen display canvas size (set in the CSS) and the width and height definitions for the canvas the same so the canvas renderer doesn't have to try to scale pixels. But if you're targeting devices with high pixel densities (such as Apple Retina displays), you can improve the quality of your graphics by experimenting with increasing the number of pixels in the canvas.

Sprite Rendering

We can't use background images and position offsets to render bubble sprites, as we did with our DOM-based system. Instead, we need to draw the bubble sprites as images onto the canvas. Remember that the sprite image file contains all four bubble colors in both resting and popping states. For example, in the sprite image shown in Figure 6-2, if we want to draw a blue bubble onto the board, we are interested in only the section of the image surrounded by the dotted line. To select only this part of the image, we'll use the clip parameters that can be passed into the drawImage method of a canvas context.

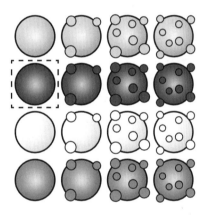

Figure 6-2: Clip boundary required to draw a blue bubble onto the board

If we want to draw the bubble in the first stage of being popped, we would move the clip area to the right. This is similar to the way we display bubbles in the DOM version except that, rather than letting the boundaries of a div element define the clip boundaries, we'll specify them in JavaScript.

To draw a clipped image to the canvas, add a couple more parameters to the drawImage method. Previously, we used drawImage with only three parameters (the Image object and *x*- and *y*-coordinates), but we can pass it a few more to clip the image. The full set of parameters that drawImage accepts are these:

```
context.drawImage(img,sx,sy,swidth,sheight,x,y,width,height);
```

The parameters are as follows:

`img`   The Image object.

`sx and sy`   The *x*- and *y*-coordinates at which to clip the image relative to the image's origin. For a blue bubble in its nonpopping state, these values would be 0 and 50, respectively.

`swidth and sheight`   The width and height of the clip area. For our bubble sprite sheet, these values will both be 50.

`x and y`   The coordinates to draw the image on the canvas relative to the canvas context origin.

`width and height`   The width and height of the image to draw. We can use these parameters to scale an image, or we can omit them if we want the image to be drawn at 1:1.

For example, to draw the blue bubble highlighted in Figure 6-2 at the coordinates (200,150) on the canvas, we would use the following:

```
$("#canvas").get(0).getContext("2d").drawImage(spriteSheet,0,50,50,50,200,150,
50,50);
```

This line of code assumes the sprite `Image` object is named `spriteSheet` and the sprite is 50 pixels wide and 50 pixels high.

Defining and Maintaining States

In the DOM-based version of the game code, we don't have to think about bubble state; we just queue up events with timeouts and animate/callback chains. Once a bubble is drawn to the screen at a fixed position, we leave it as is unless we need to change it. The bubble will be drawn in the same spot until we tell the browser to do something else with it.

But when we switch to canvas rendering, we need to render each bubble, with the correct sprite, on each frame redraw. Our code must track the state of all bubbles on the screen, whether they're moving, popping, falling, or just stationary. Each `bubble` object will track its current state and how long it's been in that state. We need that duration for when we draw the frames of the popping animation. The `Board` object currently keeps track of bubbles in the main layout, and we need to add to it so we can also keep track of those bubbles that are popping, falling, or firing.

Preparing the State Machine

To maintain bubble state, we'll first create a set of constants that refer to a bubble's state. This is referred to as using a *state machine*, which you're likely to find increasingly useful as the complexity of your games increases. The basic principles of using a state machine, as related to this game, are as follows:

- A bubble can exist in a number of states, such as moving, popping, or falling.

- The way a bubble reacts in the game will depend on the state it's in. For example, we don't want the bubble being fired to collide with a bubble being popped.

- The way a bubble is displayed may depend on its state, particularly if it's being popped.

- A bubble can be in only one state at a time; it can't be popped and popping at the same time, or popping and falling simultaneously.

Once we have the state machine set up, we'll know what we need to do to a bubble in any given situation. Some changes of state occur as a result of a user's actions, such as when they fire the bubble, but we'll also store the timestamp when a bubble enters a state. As a result, we can determine when the bubble should be moved from one state to another automatically, such as when we're in the process of popping it after a collision.

NOTE *In general, even if you think your game will be relatively simple, it's worth using a state machine as a way to manage complexity that you may not have thought of yet.*

Add the following to *bubble.js*:

bubble.js
```
var BubbleShoot = window.BubbleShoot || {};
BubbleShoot.Bubble = (function($){
❶   BubbleShoot.BubbleState = {
       CURRENT : 1,
       ON_BOARD : 2,
       FIRING : 3,
       POPPING : 4,
       FALLING : 5,
       POPPED : 6,
       FIRED : 7,
       FALLEN : 8
     };
     var Bubble = function(row,col,type,sprite){
       var that = this;
❷       var state;
       var stateStart = Date.now();
       this.getState = function(){ return state;};
❸       this.setState = function(stateIn){
         state = stateIn;
❹         stateStart = Date.now();
       };
❺       this.getTimeInState = function(){
         return Date.now() - stateStart;
       };
       --snip--
     };
     Bubble.create = function(rowNum,colNum,type){
       --snip--
     };
     return Bubble;
})(jQuery);
```

These additions allow us to store and retrieve the bubble's current state ❷, which will be one of the eight states at the top of the class ❶. Whenever we change a bubble's state ❸, we also record the timestamp when it entered that state ❹. Once we determine how long the bubble has been in its current state ❺, we can work out what to draw. For example, the amount of time a bubble has spent in the POPPING state determines which frame of the popping sequence to display.

Implementing States

Each bubble can have one of the following states, which we'll need to implement:

CURRENT	Waiting to be fired.
ON_BOARD	Already part of the board display.
FIRING	Moving toward the board or off the screen.
POPPING	Being popped. This will display one of the popping animation frames.
FALLING	An orphaned bubble that's falling from the screen.
POPPED	Done POPPING. A popped bubble doesn't need to be rendered.
FIRED	Missed the board display after FIRING. A fired bubble doesn't need to be rendered.
FALLEN	Done FALLING off the screen. A fallen bubble doesn't need to be rendered.

The bubbles displayed in the board at the beginning of a level start out in the ON_BOARD state, but all other bubbles will start in the CURRENT state and move into one of the other states, as shown in Figure 6-3.

We'll add a couple of arrays to Game to keep track of those. At the top of the class, add:

game.js
```
var BubbleShoot = window.BubbleShoot || {};
BubbleShoot.Game = (function($){
  var Game = function(){
    var curBubble;
    var board;
    var numBubbles;
❶    var bubbles = [];
    var MAX_BUBBLES = 70;
    this.init = function(){
      --snip--
    };
    var startGame = function(){
      $(".but_start_game").unbind("click");
      numBubbles = MAX_BUBBLES
      BubbleShoot.ui.hideDialog();
      board = new BubbleShoot.Board();
❷      bubbles = board.getBubbles();
      curBubble = getNextBubble();
```

```
        BubbleShoot.ui.drawBoard(board);
        $("#game").bind("click",clickGameScreen);
      };
      var getNextBubble = function(){
        var bubble = BubbleShoot.Bubble.create();
❸      bubbles.push(bubble);
❹      bubble.setState(BubbleShoot.BubbleState.CURRENT);
        bubble.getSprite().addClass("cur_bubble");
        $("#board").append(bubble.getSprite());
        BubbleShoot.ui.drawBubblesRemaining(numBubbles);
        numBubbles--;
        return bubble;
      };
      --snip--
    };
    return Game;
})(jQuery);
```

This new array ❶ will contain all of the bubbles in the game, both on and off the board layout. Initially, every bubble is part of the board, so the board contents can be used to populate the array ❷. Each time we call getNextBubble, the bubble that's ready to fire needs to be added ❸ and have its state set to CURRENT ❹.

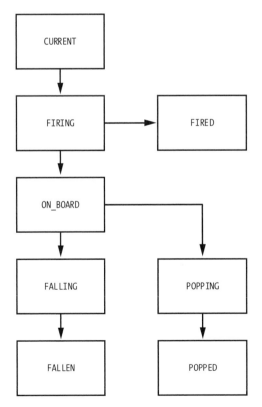

Figure 6-3: Flowchart showing bubble states

board.getBubbles is a new method that will return all of the bubbles in the rows and columns of the board as a single flat array, so add it to *board.js*:

board.js
```
var BubbleShoot = window.BubbleShoot || {};
BubbleShoot.Board = (function($){
  var NUM_ROWS = 9;
  var NUM_COLS = 32;
  var Board = function(){
    var that = this;
    --snip--
    this.getBubbles = function(){
      var bubbles = [];
      var rows = this.getRows();
      for(var i=0;i<rows.length;i++){
        var row = rows[i];
        for(var j=0;j<row.length;j++){
          var bubble = row[j];
          if(bubble){
            bubbles.push(bubble);
          };
        };
      };
      return bubbles;
    };
    return this;
  };
  --snip--
  return Board;
})(jQuery);
```

We also need to set the state of bubbles that are on the board to ON_BOARD, so make this change to the createLayout function in the same file:

```
var BubbleShoot = window.BubbleShoot || {};
BubbleShoot.Board = (function($){
  var NUM_ROWS = 9;
  var NUM_COLS = 32;
  var Board = function(){
    --snip--
  };
  var createLayout = function(){
    var rows = [];
    for(var i=0;i<NUM_ROWS;i++){
      var row = [];
      var startCol = i%2 == 0 ? 1 : 0;
      for(var j=startCol;j<NUM_COLS;j+=2){
        var bubble = BubbleShoot.Bubble.create(i,j);
        bubble.setState(BubbleShoot.BubbleState.ON_BOARD);
        row[j] = bubble;
      };
      rows.push(row);
    };
    return rows;
  };
```

```
        return Board;
})(jQuery);
```

`bubble.setState` handles the setup, which contains the states of `CURRENT` and `ON_BOARD`, but we also need to be able to change the state of a bubble.

The two states of `FIRING` and `FIRED` will be set inside `fireBubble` in *ui.js*. Amend the function as follows:

ui.js
```
var BubbleShoot = window.BubbleShoot || {};
BubbleShoot.ui = (function($){
  var ui = {
    --snip--
    fireBubble : function(bubble,coords,duration){
❶    bubble.setState(BubbleShoot.BubbleState.FIRING);
      var complete = function(){
        if(typeof(bubble.getRow()) !== undefined){
          bubble.getSprite().css(Modernizr.prefixed("transition"),"");
          bubble.getSprite().css({
            left : bubble.getCoords().left - ui.BUBBLE_DIMS/2,
            top : bubble.getCoords().top - ui.BUBBLE_DIMS/2
          });
❷        bubble.setState(BubbleShoot.BubbleState.ON_BOARD);
        }else{
❸        bubble.setState(BubbleShoot.BubbleState.FIRED);
        };
        --snip--
    },
    --snip--
  };
  return ui;
} )(jQuery);
```

When the bubble is initially fired, we set the state to `FIRING` ❶. If the bubble reaches the board, we set it to `ON_BOARD` ❷, but if it hasn't settled into a row and column, that means it missed the board, in which case it becomes `FIRED` ❸.

The other states will be set in *game.js*:

game.js
```
var Game = function(){
  --snip--
  var popBubbles = function(bubbles,delay){
    $.each(bubbles,function(){
      var bubble = this;
      setTimeout(function(){
❶      bubble.setState(BubbleShoot.BubbleState.POPPING);
        bubble.animatePop();
❷      setTimeout(function(){
          bubble.setState(BubbleShoot.BubbleState.POPPED);
        },200);
      },delay);
      board.popBubbleAt(bubble.getRow(),bubble.getCol());
      delay += 60;
    });
  };
```

```
      var dropBubbles = function(bubbles,delay){
        $.each(bubbles,function(){
          var bubble = this;
          board.popBubbleAt(bubble.getRow(),bubble.getCol());
          setTimeout(function(){
❸          bubble.setState(BubbleShoot.BubbleState.FALLING);
            bubble.getSprite().kaboom({
              callback : function(){
                bubble.getSprite().remove();
❹              bubble.setState(BubbleShoot.BubbleState.FALLEN);
              }
            })
          },delay);
        });
      };
    };
```

In popBubbles, we set every bubble to POPPING ❶, and then after 200 milliseconds, when the popping animation has finished, we set them to POPPED ❷. In dropBubbles, we set them to FALLING ❸, and then when they've finished falling at the end of the kaboom process, they become FALLEN ❹.

Now that bubbles know which state they're in at any point in the game, we can start to render them onto a canvas.

Sprite Sheets and the Canvas

We can use the existing sprite sheet PNG (*bubble_sprite_sheet.png*) from the CSS version of the game when we draw to the canvas, although we need to work with it in a different way. Rather than shifting the sprite sheet around like a background image, we'll draw part of the image that shows the correct bubble in the correct animation state. Our loading sequence will also change because we need to make sure that the sprite image is loaded before starting the game.

We'll make a new object called Renderer to handle drawing to the canvas, and we'll give it its own init method, which will preload the sprite sheet, and call that method within game.init.

Change the init method in *game.js* to the following:

game.js
```
      var BubbleShoot = window.BubbleShoot || {};
      BubbleShoot.Game = (function($){
        var Game = function(){
          --snip--
          this.init = function(){
❶          if(BubbleShoot.Renderer){
❷            BubbleShoot.Renderer.init(function(){
❸              $(".but_start_game").click("click",startGame);
            });
          }else{
              $(".but_start_game").click("click",startGame);
          };
          --snip--
```

```
  };
  return Game;
})(jQuery);
```

First, we check if `BubbleShoot.Renderer` exists ❶. If the `Modernizr.canvas` test passes when we load in scripts, the object will exist; if canvas isn't supported, the object won't exist.

Then we call a `Renderer.init` method and pass it a function as its only parameter ❷. This is the function that attaches `startGame` to the New Game button ❸.

Now we need to write the `Renderer` object. In the blank *renderer.js* file, add the following code:

renderer.js

```
         var BubbleShoot = window.BubbleShoot || {};
         BubbleShoot.Renderer = (function($){
❶         var canvas;
          var context;
          var Renderer = {
❷          init : function(callback){
❸            canvas = document.createElement("canvas");
             $(canvas).addClass("game_canvas");
❹            $("#game").prepend(canvas);
❺            $(canvas).attr("width",$(canvas).width());
             $(canvas).attr("height",$(canvas).height());
             context = canvas.getContext("2d");
             callback();
           }
          };
          return Renderer;
         })(jQuery);
```

We first create variables to hold the canvas that we'll use to render the game area ❶ and a reference to its rendering context, so we don't have to call `canvas.getContext("2d")` constantly.

In the init method, we accept the callback function as a parameter ❷, create the canvas DOM element ❸, and then prepend it in the game div ❹. We also explicitly set the width and height attributes of the canvas ❺. Remember that these attributes define the number of pixels and the boundaries of the canvas internally, so for simplicity, we set them to the same dimensions as those rendered to the screen.

That will create the canvas element for us and prime a context ready to be drawn into. We need to set the width and height of game_canvas, so add the following into *main.css*:

main.css

```
.game_canvas
{
  width: 1000px;
  height: 620px;
}
```

The DOM-rendered version uses jQuery to move objects around the screen, but we won't have DOM elements to manipulate inside a canvas, so there's nothing for jQuery to work with. Hence, we'll have to keep track of the position of every bubble on the screen with new code. Much of this will happen inside the new *sprite.js* file we've created.

MULTIPLE RENDERING METHODS: TWO APPROACHES

If you need to support different rendering methods, as we are here, you can take two approaches. First, you can create a class for each rendering method and provide identical sets of methods and properties so they can be used interchangeably. This is what we're doing with *Bubble Shooter*.

Second, you can create a single class for both rendering methods and then have code inside that branches depending on which rendering method is supported. The new class may act as just a wrapper for a different class for each method. For example, for *Bubble Shooter*, we could create something like the following pseudocode:

```
BubbleShoot.SpriteWrapper = (function($){
❶    var SpriteWrapper = function(id){
        var wrappedObject;
❷      if(BubbleShoot.Renderer){
❸        wrappedObject = getSpriteObject(id);
        }else{
❹        wrappedObject = getJQueryObject(id);
        }
❺      this.position = function(){
          return wrappedObject.position();
        };
      };
      return SpriteWrapper;
    })(jQuery);
```

Here, we would pass in some kind of identifier to an object constructor ❶ and then branch the code depending on how we'll render the game ❷. We would need new functions to return either a `Sprite` ❸ or a jQuery ❹ object, which would be stored inside the class in `wrappedObject`.

From then on, if we wanted to find the position of the object, we would call the `position` method ❺ and know we would get correct data whether the object was being rendered in the DOM or on the canvas.

The main reason we're not taking this approach with *Bubble Shooter* is that we have only one type of sprite—the bubbles on the screen. These are represented well enough by the `Bubble` class, which acts as a wrapper anyway. However, if we were dealing with many different kinds of sprites, we might want to split the structure more explicitly.

We'll write *sprite.js* so that canvas sprites can be called with the same methods that we're using on jQuery sprites. The main methods we've been calling are position, width, height, and css, and if we create implementations of these in *sprite.js*, the Sprite class will look like a jQuery object as far as the rest of our code is concerned.

Add the following to *sprite.js*:

sprite.js

```
var BubbleShoot = window.BubbleShoot || {};
BubbleShoot.Sprite = (function($){
  var Sprite = function(){
    var that = this;
❶    var left;
    var top;
❷    this.position = function(){
      return {
        left : left,
        top : top
      };
    };
❸    this.setPosition = function(args){
      if(arguments.length > 1){
        return;
      };
      if(args.left !== null)
        left = args.left;
      if(args.top !== null)
        top = args.top;
    };
❹    this.css = this.setPosition;
    return this;
  };
❺  Sprite.prototype.width = function(){
    return BubbleShoot.ui.BUBBLE_DIMS;
  };
❻  Sprite.prototype.height = function(){
    return BubbleShoot.ui.BUBBLE_DIMS;
  };
❼  Sprite.prototype.removeClass = function(){};
  Sprite.prototype.addClass = function(){};
  Sprite.prototype.remove = function(){};
  Sprite.prototype.kaboom = function(){
    jQuery.fn.kaboom.apply(this);
  };
  return Sprite;
})(jQuery);
```

Here, we've created an object that implements many of the methods that we access for jQuery objects. We have left and top coordinates ❶ and a position method ❷ that returns those coordinates in the same way that a call to jQuery's position method would. The setPosition method can set the top and left coordinates ❸ or do nothing if other values are passed.

In our DOM-based version of the game, we call the css method to set the screen coordinates of an object. setPosition has been constructed to accept the same arguments as the css method, and to spare us from having to rewrite code anywhere that the css method is called and using setPosition for the canvas version, we can create a css method of Sprite and alias it to setPosition ❹.

The width ❺ and height ❻ methods return the values defined for a bubble's dimensions in *ui.js*. Finally, we define empty methods for removeClass, addClass, and remove, which maintain compatibility with a lot of our existing code ❼. Anywhere these last methods are called will not affect the display but will also not throw an error.

When a bubble is created, we need to decide whether to create a jQuery object or an instance of Sprite, depending on whether we're rendering using the DOM or canvas. We'll do this inside the bubble creation process in *bubble.js*:

bubble.js

```
var BubbleShoot = window.BubbleShoot || {};
BubbleShoot.Bubble = (function($){
  --snip--
  var Bubble = function(row,col,type,sprite){
    --snip--
  };
  Bubble.create = function(rowNum,colNum,type){
    if(!type){
      type = Math.floor(Math.random() * 4);
    };
❶    if(!BubbleShoot.Renderer){
      var sprite = $(document.createElement("div"));
      sprite.addClass("bubble");
      sprite.addClass("bubble_" + type);
    }else{
❷      var sprite = new BubbleShoot.Sprite();
    }
    var bubble = new Bubble(rowNum,colNum,type,sprite);
    return bubble;
  };
  return Bubble;
})(jQuery);
```

This code checks again that the Renderer object is loaded ❶ (which happens if canvas is enabled) and, if not, continues the DOM-based path. Otherwise, we make a new Sprite object ❷. With this in place, a call to curBubble.getSprite will return a valid object no matter whether we're using jQuery with CSS or a pure canvas route.

The last part of initializing the Sprite objects is to make sure they have the correct onscreen coordinates. In the DOM version of the game, we set these in the CSS, but with the canvas, we have to set them in JavaScript code. These will be set in the createLayout function in *board.js*:

board.js
```javascript
var BubbleShoot = window.BubbleShoot || {};
BubbleShoot.Board = (function($){
  var NUM_ROWS = 9;
  var NUM_COLS = 32;
  var Board = function(){
    --snip--
    return this;
  };
  var createLayout = function(){
    var rows = [];
    for(var i=0;i<NUM_ROWS;i++){
      var row = [];
      var startCol = i%2 == 0 ? 1 : 0;
      for(var j=startCol;j<NUM_COLS;j+=2){
        var bubble = BubbleShoot.Bubble.create(i,j);
        bubble.setState(BubbleShoot.BubbleState.ON_BOARD);
❶       if(BubbleShoot.Renderer){
❷         var left = j * BubbleShoot.ui.BUBBLE_DIMS/2;
          var top = i * BubbleShoot.ui.ROW_HEIGHT;
❸         bubble.getSprite().setPosition({
            left : left,
            top : top
          });
        };
        row[j] = bubble;
      };
      rows.push(row);
    };
    return rows;
  };
  return Board;
})(jQuery);
```

If the renderer exists ❶, we calculate the left and top coordinates of where the bubble should be displayed ❷ and then set the sprite's properties to those values ❸.

The current bubble also needs its position set, so this will happen inside getNextBubble in *game.js*:

game.js
```javascript
var BubbleShoot = window.BubbleShoot || {};
BubbleShoot.Game = (function($){
  var Game = function(){
    --snip--
    var getNextBubble = function(){
      var bubble = BubbleShoot.Bubble.create();
```

```
    bubbles.push(bubble);
    bubble.setState(BubbleShoot.BubbleState.CURRENT);
    bubble.getSprite().addClass("cur_bubble");
    var top = 470;
    var left = ($("#board").width() - BubbleShoot.ui.BUBBLE_DIMS)/2;
    bubble.getSprite().css({
      top : top,
      left : left
    });
    $("#board").append(bubble.getSprite());
    BubbleShoot.ui.drawBubblesRemaining(numBubbles);
    numBubbles--;
    return bubble;
  };
  --snip--
  };
  return Game;
})(jQuery);
```

We now have all bubble positions tracked and know their state at all times. We can also manipulate a sprite representation, but nothing will appear on the screen just yet. In the next section, we'll render our sprites to the canvas.

The Canvas Renderer

To animate anything on the canvas, we need to clear pixels before each redraw. To render the game, we'll use setTimeout with a timer to redraw the position and state of every bubble on a frame-by-frame basis. This process will be the same for just about any game you build and, certainly, for anything where the display is constantly being updated. In theory, we only need to redraw the canvas when information on the screen has changed; in practice, working out when there's new information to show can be difficult. Fortunately, canvas rendering is so fast that there's generally no reason not to just update the display as often as possible.

We'll store the value of the timeout ID returned by setTimeout so we know whether or not the frame counter is running. This will happen at the top of *game.js* in a new variable called requestAnimationID, where we'll also store a timestamp for when the last animation occurred:

game.js
```
var BubbleShoot = window.BubbleShoot || {};
var Game = function(){
  var curBubble;
  var board;
  var numBubbles;
  var bubbles = [];
  var MAX_BUBBLES = 70;
❶ var requestAnimationID;
  this.init = function(){
  };
  --snip--
```

```
                var startGame = function(){
                  $(".but_start_game").unbind("click");
                  $("#board .bubble").remove();
                  numBubbles = MAX_BUBBLES;
                  BubbleShoot.ui.hideDialog();
                  board = new BubbleShoot.Board();
                  bubbles = board.getBubbles();
  ❷             if(BubbleShoot.Renderer)
                {
                    if(!requestAnimationID)
  ❸                   requestAnimationID = setTimeout(renderFrame,40);
                  }else{
                    BubbleShoot.ui.drawBoard(board);
                  };
                  curBubble = getNextBubble(board);
                  $("#game").bind("click",clickGameScreen);
                };
              };
              return Game;
            })(jQuery);
```

We add the two variables ❶, and if the Renderer object exists ❷, we start the timeout running to draw the first animation frame ❸.

We haven't written renderFrame yet, but before we do, we'll write a method in *renderer.js* to draw all of the bubbles. The method will accept an array of bubble objects as an input.

First we need to load the bubble images into *renderer.js*:

renderer.js

```
            var BubbleShoot = window.BubbleShoot || {};
            BubbleShoot.Renderer = (function($){
              var canvas;
              var context;
  ❶           var spriteSheet;
  ❷           var BUBBLE_IMAGE_DIM = 50;
              var Renderer = {
                init : function(callback){
                  canvas = document.createElement("canvas");
                  $(canvas).addClass("game_canvas");
                  $("#game").prepend(canvas);
                  $(canvas).attr("width",$(canvas).width());
                  $(canvas).attr("height",$(canvas).height());
                  context = canvas.getContext("2d");
                  spriteSheet = new Image();
  ❸               spriteSheet.src = "_img/bubble_sprite_sheet.png";
  ❹               spriteSheet.onload = function() {
                    callback();
                  };
                }
              };
              return Renderer;
            })(jQuery);
```

We create a variable to hold the image data ❶ and define another variable for the width and height of each bubble image ❷. The dimensions will tell us where to crop each image within the sprite sheet. We then load in the image file ❸, and the callback function that's passed into init is triggered after the image has loaded ❹.

Next we'll create the function to draw the sprites onto the canvas.

renderer.js

```
var BubbleShoot = window.BubbleShoot || {};
BubbleShoot.Renderer = (function($){
  --snip--
  var Renderer = {
    init : function(callback){
      --snip--
    },
❶  render : function(bubbles){
      context.clearRect(0,0,canvas.width,canvas.height);
      context.translate(120,0);
❷    $.each(bubbles,function(){
        var bubble = this;
❸      var clip = {
          top : bubble.getType() * BUBBLE_IMAGE_DIM,
          left : 0
        };
❹      Renderer.drawSprite(bubble.getSprite(),clip);
      });
      context.translate(-120,0);
    },
    drawSprite : function(sprite,clip){
❺    context.translate(sprite.position().left + sprite.width()/2,sprite.
        position().top + sprite.height()/2);
❻    context.drawImage(spriteSheet,clip.left,clip.top,BUBBLE_IMAGE_DIM,
        BUBBLE_IMAGE_DIM,-sprite.width()/2,-sprite.height()/2,BUBBLE_IMAGE_
        DIM,BUBBLE_IMAGE_DIM);
❼    context.translate(-sprite.position().left - sprite.width()/2,
        -sprite.position().top - sprite.height()/2);
    }
  };
  return Renderer;
})(jQuery);
```

First, we create a render method that accepts an array of Bubble objects ❶. We then clear the canvas and offset the context by 120 pixels so the board display is drawn in the center of the screen. The code then loops over each bubble in the array ❷ and defines an (x,y) coordinate from which to extract the bubble's sprite from the image ❸. The x-coordinate always starts at zero until we add frames for the popping animation, and the y-coordinate is the bubble type (0 to 3) multiplied by the height of a bubble image (50 pixels). We pass this information along with the bubble's Sprite object to another new method called drawSprite ❹ before resetting the context position.

Inside `drawSprite`, we translate the context ❺ by the coordinates of the sprite, remembering to offset the (top,left) coordinates by half of (width,height) to get the center of the image, and then draw the image ❻. In general, it's best to translate the canvas context so its origin is at the center of any image being drawn, because the `rotate` method of the context performs rotations around the context origin. This means that if we want to rotate an image around its center, we already have the context set up correctly to do so.

Finally, after calling `drawImage`, we translate the context back to the origin ❼. To see the board being rendered to the canvas, we just need to put `renderFrame` into *game.js*:

game.js

```
var BubbleShoot = window.BubbleShoot || {};
  var Game = function(){
    --snip--
    var renderFrame = function(){
      BubbleShoot.Renderer.render(bubbles);
      requestAnimationID = setTimeout(renderFrame,40);
    };
  };
  return Game;
})(jQuery);
```

Reload the page in your browser to start the game again. After clicking New Game, you should see the board render in its initial state. However, firing a bubble produces no animation, and neither does popping, falling, or anything else. In the next section, we'll get bubble firing working again and also animate the bubble popping. If you open the game in a browser that doesn't support canvas, then the game will still work as before because we have left the DOM version intact. Next, we'll add animation to the canvas version.

Moving Sprites on the Canvas

With the CSS version of the game, we used jQuery to move objects around on the screen with one call to the `animate` method. For canvas animation, we need to calculate and update movements manually.

The process of animating on the canvas is the same as jQuery's internal processes, and we'll give `Sprite` an `animate` method so we can continue to use our existing code. The `animate` method will do the following:

1. Accept destination coordinates for a bubble and the duration of the movement.

2. Move the object a small distance toward those coordinates by a value proportional to the time elapsed since the last frame.

3. Repeat step 2 until the bubble reaches its destination.

This process is identical to the one that happens when we use jQuery's animate method and is one you'll use just about any time you want to move an object around the screen.

The renderFrame method, which is already called during each frame, will run the entire animation process. After the bubble sprites calculate their own coordinates, renderFrame will trigger the drawing process. We'll add an animate method to the Sprite object so our existing game logic will work without us having to rewrite our code. Remember that when we call animate in *ui.js*, we pass in two parameters:

- An object specifying left and top position coordinates
- An object specifying duration, callback function, and easing

By constructing the animate method of Sprite to take the same parameters, we can avoid making any changes to the call in *ui.js*. Add the following to *sprite.js*:

sprite.js
```
var BubbleShoot = window.BubbleShoot || {};
BubbleShoot.Sprite = (function($){
  var Sprite = function(){
    --snip--
    this.css = function(args){
      --snip--
    };
❶    this.animate = function(destination,config){
❷      var duration = config.duration;
❸      var animationStart = Date.now();
❹      var startPosition = that.position();
❺      that.updateFrame = function(){
        var elapsed = Date.now() - animationStart;
        var proportion = elapsed/duration;
        if(proportion > 1)
          proportion = 1;
❻        var posLeft = startPosition.left + (destination.left - startPosition.
          left) * proportion;
        var posTop = startPosition.top + (destination.top - startPosition.top)
          * proportion;
❼        that.css({
          left : posLeft,
          top : posTop
        });
      };
❽      setTimeout(function(){
❾        that.updateFrame = null;
❿        if(config.complete)
          config.complete();
      },duration);
    };
    return this;
  };
  --snip--
  return Sprite;
})(jQuery);
```

The destination parameter passed into animate ❶ represents the sprite's destination coordinates, which are contained in an object that looks like this:

```
{top: 100,left: 100}
```

We also pass a configuration object, which will have a duration property ❷, plus an optional post-animation callback function to run when the animation is over.

Next, we set a start time for the animation ❸ and store the starting position ❹. These will both be used to calculate a bubble's position at any time.

We dynamically add the updateFrame method onto the Sprite object ❺ so we can call it each frame to recalculate a bubble's position. Inside updateFrame, we calculate how much of the animation is completed. In case the last timeout is called after the animation has completed, we ensure that the proportion is never greater than 1 so that a bubble never moves past its target destination. The new coordinates are calculated ❻ with the following equations:

$$\text{current } x = \text{start } x + (\text{final } x - \text{start } x) \times \text{proportion elapsed}$$

$$\text{current } y = \text{start } y + (\text{final } y - \text{start } y) \times \text{proportion elapsed}$$

Once we have the new top and left coordinates, the position of the sprite is updated with a call to its css method ❼. We don't need updateFrame to run when the object has finished moving, so a timeout call is set ❽ to remove the method after duration ❾ passes, which is when the animation will be complete. This also calls any post-animation function that was passed in as the callback property of the config variable ❿.

Now that we can calculate a bubble's new coordinates, add a call to updateFrame in *game.js*:

game.js
```
var BubbleShoot = window.BubbleShoot || {};
  var Game = function(){
    --snip--
    var renderFrame = function(){
❶    $.each(bubbles,function(){
❷      if(this.getSprite().updateFrame)
❸        this.getSprite().updateFrame();
      });
      BubbleShoot.Renderer.render(bubbles);
      requestAnimationID = setTimeout(renderFrame,40);
    };
  };
  return Game;
})(jQuery);
```

Each time renderFrame is called on a bubble ❶, if the method updateFrame is defined ❷, we call that method ❸.

We also need to call `animate` in `fireBubble` in *ui.js* by checking for the existence of `BubbleShoot.Renderer` again. We know that `BubbleShoot.Renderer` will exist only if canvas is supported, and we want to use the canvas for rendering if that is the case. The outcome is that CSS transitions will animate the bubbles only if CSS transitions are supported *and* canvas rendering isn't supported.

ui.js
```
var BubbleShoot = window.BubbleShoot || {};
BubbleShoot.ui = (function($){
  var ui = {
    --snip--
    fireBubble : function(bubble,coords,duration){
      --snip--
      if(Modernizr.csstransitions && !BubbleShoot.Renderer){
        --snip--
      }else{
        --snip--
      }
    },
    --snip--
  };
  return ui;
} )(jQuery);
```

Reload the game and fire away! You should now have a working game again, but this time all the images are rendered onto the canvas. But now there's no popping animation because we're not handling changes in bubble state in the display. The game state is internally correct, but the screen isn't entirely in sync because we never see a bubble popping. Rendering the bubbles in their correct state is the focus of the next section.

Animating Canvas Sprite Frames

Currently, every bubble is rendered in the same visual state regardless of whether it's sitting in the board, popping, newly fired, and so on. Bubbles remain on the screen after they've been popped, and we're missing out on the popping animation! This happens because bubbles are never deleted from the `bubbles` array in `Game`, so they're rendered even after they've been deleted from the `Board` object.

We already know which state a bubble is in, and we have the sprite sheet image loaded into memory to access all of the animation states. Drawing the correct state involves making sure that the `drawSprite` method of `Renderer` is either called with the correct state for a visible bubble or skipped entirely for any bubbles that have been popped or dropped off the screen. The changes in a bubble's appearance that we need to implement are listed by state in Table 6-1.

Table 6-1: Visual Changes Based on Bubble State

Bubble's state in code	Visual displayed to the player
CURRENT_BUBBLE	No change
ON_BOARD	No change
FIRING	No change
POPPING	Render one of four bubble frames, depending on how long the bubble has been POPPING
FALLING	No change
POPPED	Skip rendering
FALLEN	Skip rendering
FIRED	Skip rendering

Those changes will happen inside `Renderer.render`. We'll loop over the entire bubble array and either skip the rendering stage or adjust the coordinates to clip the sprite sheet for the correct stage in the popping animation. Make the following change to *renderer.js*:

renderer.js
```
var BubbleShoot = window.BubbleShoot || {};
BubbleShoot.Renderer = (function($){
  --snip--
  var Renderer = {
    init : function(callback){
      --snip--
    },
    render : function(bubbles){
      bubbles.each(function(){
        var bubble = this;
        var clip = {
          top : bubble.getType() * BUBBLE_IMAGE_DIM,
          left : 0
        };
❶       switch(bubble.getState()){
          case BubbleShoot.BubbleState.POPPING:
❷           var timeInState = bubble.getTimeInState();
❸           if(timeInState < 80){
              clip.left = BUBBLE_IMAGE_DIM;
❹           }else if(timeInState < 140){
              clip.left = BUBBLE_IMAGE_DIM*2;
❺           }else{
              clip.left = BUBBLE_IMAGE_DIM*3;
            };
            break;
❻         case BubbleShoot.BubbleState.POPPED:
            return;
❼         case BubbleShoot.BubbleState.FIRED:
            return;
❽         case BubbleShoot.BubbleState.FALLEN:
            return;
        }
```

```
❾              Renderer.drawSprite(bubble.getSprite(),clip);
           });
         },
         drawSprite : function(sprite,clip){
           --snip--
         }
       };
       return Renderer;
    })(jQuery);
```

First, we want to see which state the bubble is in ❶. To do this, we'll use a switch statement. State machines are often written using switch/case statements rather than multiple if/else statements. Using this structure not only makes it easier to add any future states but also provides a clue to others reading the code in the future that they're looking at a state machine.

If the bubble is popping, we want to know how long it's been in that state ❷. That time determines which animation frame to fetch. We use the unpopped state for the first 80 milliseconds ❸, the first frame for the next 60 milliseconds ❹, and the final popping frame from that point until the POPPING state is cleared ❺.

If the bubble is in the POPPED ❻, FIRED ❼, or FALLEN ❽ states, we return and skip rendering altogether. Otherwise, we call drawSprite as before ❾.

Now if you reload the game, it should completely work again. Without making drastic changes, we've refactored our entire game area to use either canvas- or DOM-based rendering, depending on browser compatibility. The browser you use to load the game and the features that browser supports will determine how *Bubble Shooter* is presented to you:

- If your browser supports the canvas element, you'll see that version.

- If your browser supports CSS transitions but *not* the canvas element, you'll see the CSS transition version.

- If neither of the above is supported, you'll see the DOM version animated with jQuery.

Summary

That covers most of the core of drawing the graphics elements of an HTML5 game, whether you're using HTML and CSS or an entirely canvas-based approach. But that doesn't mean we've finished the game! We have no sound, only one level of play exists, and a scoring system would be nice. In the next chapter, we'll implement these elements and explore a few more features of HTML5, including local storage for saving game state, requestAnimationFrame for smoother animations, and how to make sound work reliably.

Further Practice

1. When bubbles pop, the animation plays identically for every bubble. Experiment with changing the timing so that some bubbles play the animation faster and some slower. Also, try adding some rotation to the bubbles as they're drawn onto the canvas. This should give the popping animation a much richer feel for very little effort.

2. When orphaned bubbles fall, they remain as the default sprite. Change *renderer.js* so that bubbles pop as they're falling.

7

LEVELS, SOUND, AND MORE

In this chapter, we'll add a few finishing touches to *Bubble Shooter* and cover a few more features of HTML5. Right now, the bubble grid could fill up the entire page in no time, giving players no room to fire bubbles. To prevent this from happening, we'll make the game end if the player adds more than two rows to the bottom of the board. We'll also implement multiple levels and high scores using the Local Storage API, smooth out animation with requestAnimationFrame, and add sound to the game with HTML5. Let's start by adding multiple levels and high scores.

Multiple Levels and High Scores

It's possible to complete a level by clearing out all of the bubbles, but thereafter, if you want to play again, you must refresh the browser. Obviously, this is not satisfactory for a game, and a few other game flow elements are missing:

- A limited supply of bubbles (otherwise, the player can continue firing forever and cause the bubble counter to display negative numbers!)
- A scoring system
- End-of-level conditions
- Further levels

The game will award points for each bubble popped, and those points will add up to the player's score. We already have the information we need to limit the player's bubble supply, because we count the bubbles, although our count can go into negative numbers. To add multiple levels that increase in difficulty, we'll give the player fewer bubbles at each level.

New Game State Variables

The first steps we need to take are incorporating the bubble counter and creating other game state variables. We could create a new object to store all of the game state parameters, such as the player's score, the number of bubbles remaining, the level number, and so on. Alternatively, we could store these as variables inside the Game object. I've opted for the latter because there are only three values to track. If you need to track more information or if the information to track is more complex, it's best to store the data in its own object to keep *game.js* as small and readable as possible.

Let's add a few new variables to the top of the Game class and give the player a different number of bubbles to complete the level based on the level number:

game.js
```
var BubbleShoot = window.BubbleShoot || {};
    BubbleShoot.Game = (function($){
    var Game = function(){
      var curBubble;
      var board;
      var numBubbles;
      var bubbles = [];
      var MAX_BUBBLES = 70;
❶     var POINTS_PER_BUBBLE = 50;
❷     var level = 0;
❸     var score = 0;
❹     var highScore = 0;
```

```
        var requestAnimationID;
        this.init = function(){
          --snip--
        };
        var startGame = function(){
          $(".but_start_game").unbind("click");
          BubbleShoot.ui.hideDialog();
❺        numBubbles = MAX_BUBBLES - level * 5;
          board = new BubbleShoot.Board();
          bubbles = board.getBubbles();
          if(BubbleShoot.Renderer)
          {
            if(!requestAnimationID)
              requestAnimationID = setTimeout(renderFrame,40);
          }else{
            BubbleShoot.ui.drawBoard(board);
          };
          curBubble = getNextBubble();
          $("#game").bind("click",clickGameScreen);
        };
        --snip--
      };
      return Game;
})(jQuery);
```

We've created new variables for the number of points to award for each bubble ❶, the player's current level ❷, their current score ❸, and a high score ❹. When the game starts, we reduce the number of bubbles by 5 for every level the player has completed ❺. At the first level, players are given 70 bubbles, at level 2, they have 65, and so on.

NOTE   *You may notice a couple of problems with the way we are calculating the number of bubbles available. First, it's impossible to complete level 14, because the number of bubbles the user would be given would be zero at this point. Second, the levels leading up to this will be extremely difficult. It's hard to imagine being able to complete a level with 20 or 30 bubbles, let alone only 10 or 15! I'll leave a solution to this problem as an exercise for the end of the chapter.*

Display Level and Score

We don't have anywhere to display the score yet, so we'll add a DOM element to *index.html* for that, as well as somewhere to display the current level and high score. The bar at the top of the screen is a good place in the layout to display that information. The new elements are shown at the top of Figure 7-1.

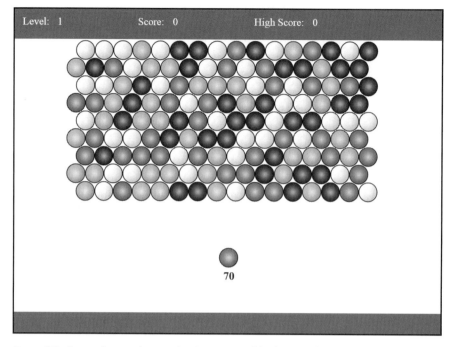

Figure 7-1: Screen layout showing level, score, and high score display

index.html

```
<!DOCTYPE HTML>
<html lang="en-US">
<head>
  --snip--
</head>
<body>
<div id="page">
  <div id="top_bar">
❶    <div id="top_level_box" class="top_bar_box">
       <div id="top_level_label">Level:</div>
       <div id="level">1</div>
     </div>
❷    <div class="top_bar_box">
       <div id="top_score_label">Score:</div>
       <div id="score">0</div>
     </div>
❸    <div class="top_bar_box">
       <div id="top_score_label">High Score:</div>
       <div id="high_score">0</div>
     </div>
  </div>
  --snip--
</div>
</body>
</html>
```

Three new <div> elements were added: one each for the level number ❶, the current game score ❷, and the high score ❸. Each <div> has an element to display the label and then a value.

These also need style definitions in *main.css*:

```
body
{
  margin: 0;
}
#page
{
  position: absolute;
  left: 0;
  top: 0;
  width: 1000px;
  height: 738px;
}
  #top_bar
  {
    position: absolute;
    left: 0;
    top: 0;
    width: 1000px;
    height: 70px;
    background-color: #369;
    color: #fff;
  }
  .top_bar_box
  {
    font-size: 24px;
    line-height: 60px;
    float: left;
    margin-left:20px;
    width: 250px;
  }
  .top_bar_box div
  {
    float: left;
    margin-right: 20px;
  }
--snip--
```

❶ `.top_bar_box`
❷ `.top_bar_box div`

I haven't styled each of the three elements individually; instead, I've given them a common class of top_bar_box ❶. The basic CSS styling gives each element a width of 250 pixels and floats it to the left, so the elements form a row at the top of the screen inside top_bar. The label and value displayed for each element is inside a <div>, so the styling for that is applied without creating a new CSS class ❷.

Now let's award some points to the player and display their score and level. Points need to be awarded and displayed whenever bubbles are popped or orphaned, and score and level values should be displayed at the start of the game. First, we need functions in *ui.js* to draw the values to the screen. We'll put them inside *ui.js* to continue to keep *game.js* free of display code:

```
var BubbleShoot = window.BubbleShoot || {};
BubbleShoot.ui = (function($){
  --snip--
  var ui = {
    --snip--
❶   drawScore : function(score){
      $("#score").text(score);
    },
❷   drawHighScore : function(highScore){
      $("#high_score").text(highScore);
    },
❸   drawLevel : function(level){
      $("#level").text(level+1);
    }
  };
  --snip--
  return ui;
} )(jQuery);
```

drawScore ❶ and drawHighScore ❷ accept score values and draw them into the relevant <div>s on the screen. drawLevel writes the level number but adds 1 to it first, because the internal level state starts at zero ❸. Although all three of these functions contain only a single line of code, it's a good idea to create separate functions for them and write, for example, ui.drawScore(score) rather than $("#score").text(score) each time you update the score value. Then, if you want to add visual effects to any of the elements when they change, you can do so in one function without tracking down every instance where the score is updated. If you want the score to flash, say, every time it increases, then you would only need to make the change in one place.

Now we add calls to these functions into *game.js* within startGame and clickScreen:

```
var BubbleShoot = window.BubbleShoot || {};
  BubbleShoot.Game = (function($){
  var Game = function(){
    --snip--
    var startGame = function(){
      $(".but_start_game").unbind("click");
      BubbleShoot.ui.hideDialog();
      numBubbles = MAX_BUBBLES;
      board = new BubbleShoot.Board();
      bubbles = board.getBubbles();
      if(BubbleShoot.Renderer)
      {
        if(!requestAnimationID)
          requestAnimationID = setTimeout(renderFrame,40);
```

```
        }else{
          BubbleShoot.ui.drawBoard(board);
        };
        curBubble = getNextBubble();
        $("#game").bind("click",clickGameScreen);
❶      BubbleShoot.ui.drawScore(score);
        BubbleShoot.ui.drawLevel(level);
      };
      var clickGameScreen = function(e){
        var angle = BubbleShoot.ui.getBubbleAngle(curBubble.getSprite(),e,board.
          calculateTop());
        var duration = 750;
        var distance = 1000;
        var collision = BubbleShoot.CollisionDetector.findIntersection(curBubble,
          board,angle);
        if(collision){
          var coords = collision.coords;
          duration = Math.round(duration * collision.distToCollision / distance);
          board.addBubble(curBubble,coords);
          var group = board.getGroup(curBubble,{});
          if(group.list.length >= 3){
            popBubbles(group.list,duration);
            var orphans = board.findOrphans();
            var delay = duration + 200 + 30 * group.list.length;
            dropBubbles(orphans,delay);
❷          var popped = [].concat(group.list,orphans);
❸          var points = popped.length * POINTS_PER_BUBBLE;
❹          score += points;
❺          setTimeout(function(){
              BubbleShoot.ui.drawScore(score);
            },delay);
          };
        }else{
          --snip--
        };
        --snip--
      };
      --snip--
    };
    return Game;
})(jQuery);
```

We draw the score and level at game start ❶. When bubbles are popped,
we first want to make a set of all of the bubbles that are both popped and
orphaned. This is done by concatenating two arrays—the popped list and
orphaned list ❷—and then multiplying POINTS_PER_BUBBLE by the length of
the new array ❸. We then increment the score internally ❹, but we only
update the display once the bubble has finished firing at the end of delay ❺.
If you reload and start the game, your score should now increment.

Next, we'll check for the end game conditions. Two states could result
in the end game being reached: the player could run out of bubbles to fire,

or the player could pop all the bubbles in the game board. If the former, then we want to show players a final score and have them start a new game at the first level. If the latter, then we want to clear the board, increment the level number, and prompt to start the next level.

We know that game state only changes as a result of the player firing a bubble, so the only place we need to check for possible end game conditions is after we calculate the result of any collision. We'll do this immediately after the bubble has been fired, which happens inside `clickGameScreen` inside `Game`. If the board is empty or the player has run out of bubbles, we'll end the game; if not, we'll give the player the next bubble to fire. Make the following change to *game.js*:

game.js
```
var BubbleShoot = window.BubbleShoot || {};
  BubbleShoot.Game = (function($){
  var Game = function(){
    --snip--
    var clickGameScreen = function(e){
      --snip--
      BubbleShoot.ui.fireBubble(curBubble,coords,duration);
❶    if(numBubbles == 0){
        endGame(false);
❷    }else if(board.isEmpty()){
        endGame(true);
❸    }else{
        curBubble = getNextBubble(board);
      }
    };
    --snip--
  };
  return Game;
})(jQuery);
```

We first check to see if the player has run out of bubbles ❶ and then check to see if the board is cleared of bubbles ❷. If neither is true, we retrieve the next bubble as usual ❸. A new function called `endGame` uses a Boolean to determine whether the player has won or lost the level: `false` means the player lost (by running out of bubbles), and `true` means the player won (by clearing the board).

Note the call to `board.isEmpty`, which is a method that we haven't written yet. Let's do that now by adding the following into the *board.js* class:

board.js
```
var BubbleShoot = window.BubbleShoot || {};
BubbleShoot.Board = (function($){
  var NUM_ROWS = 9;
  var NUM_COLS = 32;
  var Board = function(){
    var that = this;
    --snip--
```

```
      this.isEmpty = function(){
        return this.getBubbles().length == 0;
      };
      return this;
    };
    --snip--
    return Board;
})(jQuery);
```

The isEmpty function checks to see if a call to the getBubbles method returns any objects. If the array has a length of zero, all the bubbles have been popped.

The second possible end game condition is if the player adds more than two new rows to the bottom of the board. We already have a function, getRows, to return the array of rows, so we just need to check whether its length is greater than the maximum number of rows we'll permit, which is 11.

game.js
```
var BubbleShoot = window.BubbleShoot || {};
BubbleShoot.Game = (function($){
var Game = function(){
var curBubble;
var board;
var numBubbles;
var bubbles = [];
var MAX_BUBBLES = 70;
var POINTS_PER_BUBBLE = 50;
❶  var MAX_ROWS = 11;
     --snip--
     var clickGameScreen = function(e){
       --snip--
       BubbleShoot.ui.fireBubble(curBubble,coords,duration);
❷      if(board.getRows().length > MAX_ROWS){
         endGame(false);
       }else if(numBubbles == 0){
         endGame(false);
       }else if(board.isEmpty()){
         endGame(true);
       }else{
         curBubble = getNextBubble(board);
       }
     };
     --snip--
   };
   return Game;
})(jQuery);
```

To make the code easy to read, we'll store the maximum number of rows allowed in a variable called MAX_ROWS ❶ and then we'll check to see whether the number of rows on the board is greater than this number ❷; if so, we'll end the game.

We also need to display messages to the player indicating a win or loss, a score, and so on. If we have a large number of different messages to show, we might create some JavaScript code to dynamically create and display dialogs. But we only have a couple of variations, so we'll hardcode them into the HTML. The dialog we'll show will look the same as the one for starting the game but with more information, as shown in Figure 7-2.

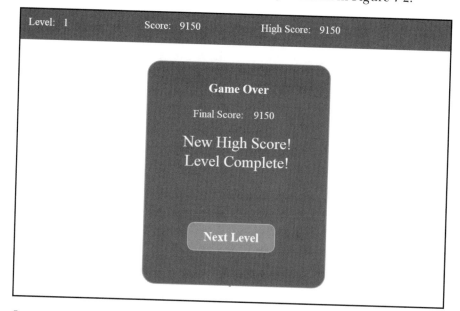

Figure 7-2: The end game dialog

Let's add the structure for this to *index.html* now:

index.html
```
<!DOCTYPE HTML>
<html lang="en-US">
<head>
  --snip--
</head>
<body>
<div id="page">
  --snip--
  <div id="start_game" class="dialog">
    <div id="start_game_message">
      <h2>Start a new game</h2>
    </div>
    <div class="but_start_game button">
      New Game
    </div>
  </div>
❶ <div id="end_game" class="dialog">
    <div id="end_game_message">
      <h2>Game Over</h2>
❷     <div id="final_score">
        <span>Final Score:</span>
```

```
            <span id="final_score_value"></span>
          </div>
❸        <div id="new_high_score">New High Score!</div>
❹        <div id="level_failed" class="level_failed">Level Failed!</div>
❺        <div id="level_complete" class="level_complete">Level Complete!</div>
        </div>
❻      <div class="but_start_game button">
❼        <span class="level_complete">Next Level</span>
❽        <span class="level_failed">New Game</span>
        </div>
      </div>
    </div>
    </body>
    </html>
```

Our game only ever shows one dialog ❶, which contains a message for the final score ❷, whether the level was completed or failed. If the player reaches a new high score, we'll show that message ❸. The Level Failed! ❹ or Level Complete! ❺ messages will be shown depending on the situation. Finally, a single button will enable the next game to start ❻, which will lead to either the next level ❼ or a brand-new game ❽. We can determine after the button has been clicked whether the game is being restarted or continued, because we'll know the current level number.

When we show the end_game dialog, we'll show or hide the level_complete or level_failed classes, as appropriate, to display the correct messages. Notice that the level_complete class is attached to both the Level Complete! message ❺ and the Next Level button ❼, whereas the level_failed class is attached to the Level Failed! message ❹ and the New Game button ❽. This will enable us to, for example, hide all of the level_failed elements with a single jQuery call:

```
$(".level_failed").hide();
```

This is one of the advantages of using HTML and CSS for the user interface, and it's possible because *Bubble Shooter* is a relatively simple game. But even if you had a much larger range of messages to show in a dialog, you could still use jQuery to create DOM elements and use CSS to style them.

The dialog will inherit some styling from the dialog class definition, but we need to add some more definitions to *main.css*:

main.css
```
#final_score
{
  margin: 26px 0;
}
  #end_game_message span
  {
    margin-right: 20px;
    font-size: 24px;
  }
```

```css
#level_complete,#level_failed,#new_high_score
{
  font-size: 36px;
  color: #fff;
}
```

We now want to create the endGame function in *game.js*. This will display the end-of-game dialog with the appropriate win or lose message and then allow the player to either play the next level or start a new game:

```javascript
var BubbleShoot = window.BubbleShoot || {};
BubbleShoot.Game = (function($){
  var Game = function(){
    --snip--
    var renderFrame = function(){
      --snip--
    };
    var endGame = function(hasWon){
❶      if(score > highScore){
❷        highScore = score;
❸        $("#new_high_score").show();
❹        BubbleShoot.ui.drawHighScore(highScore);
      }else{
❺        $("#new_high_score").hide();
      };
❻      if(hasWon){
        level++;
❼      }else{
        score = 0;
        level = 0;
      };
❽      $(".but_start_game").click("click",startGame);
❾      $("#board .bubble").remove();
      BubbleShoot.ui.endGame(hasWon,score);
    };
  };
  return Game;
})(jQuery);
```

First, we check to see if the player's score is higher than the value of highScore, which starts at zero ❶. If so, highScore is updated ❷ and we show the new_high_score element inside the game completion dialog ❸. Then a call to ui.drawHighScore occurs, which we created when we updated the in-game scoring display ❹. If there isn't a new high score, the message is hidden ❺.

The next branch checks if the player has won and, if so ❻, increments level by 1. If the player lost, score and level are reset to zero ❼. Then we need to enable the startGame button again by binding the click event to it ❽, clear the rest of the bubbles from the display ❾, and call a new method in *ui.js* that will display the game over dialog.

Note that it doesn't matter whether the player is playing the first level or the fiftieth, because startGame just draws the current level and starts the game; therefore, we don't need to create a new function to handle new levels.

But the display isn't the only part of the game that should react to a game over. The player shouldn't be able to shoot bubbles anymore either! Let's also create a function called endGame in *ui.js*. Whereas endGame in *game.js* deals with the game logic aspects to finishing a level, the code in *ui.js* will handle the visual aspects of ending the game, such as showing the dialog and populating it with the player's score:

<table>
<tr><td>*ui.js*</td><td>

```
var BubbleShoot = window.BubbleShoot || {};
BubbleShoot.ui = (function($){
  --snip--
  var ui = {
    --snip--
    endGame : function(hasWon,score){
      $("#game").unbind("click");
      BubbleShoot.ui.drawBubblesRemaining(0);
      if(hasWon){
        $(".level_complete").show();
        $(".level_failed").hide();
      }else{
        $(".level_complete").hide();
        $(".level_failed").show();
      };
      $("#end_game").fadeIn(500);
      $("#final_score_value").text(score);
    }
  };
  --snip--
  return ui;
} )(jQuery);
```

</td></tr>
</table>

The markers ❶ ❷ ❸ appear beside `$("#game").unbind("click");`, `BubbleShoot.ui.drawBubblesRemaining(0);`, and `if(hasWon){` respectively; ❹ appears beside `$("#end_game").fadeIn(500);`.

When the game is finished, the endGame method ensures that clicks ❶ in the game area will no longer trigger the clickGameScreen function, because we don't want the player to fire bubbles when the game is over. It also updates the bubbles remaining display to zero ❷ and shows the correct win/lose message inside the dialog ❸. Then we show the dialog with the messages for Level Complete! or Level Failed! inside ❹.

Ending Levels Efficiently

Currently, *Bubble Shooter*'s end game can be a bit tedious: the player is left firing bubbles until they form groups large enough to pop. This can also prove problematic if the bubbles don't come out in the right color combinations. For example, if the only bubble on the board is blue and the randomizer generates only red bubbles, the player might fail a level through no fault of their own! Rather than expect the player to clear every bubble, we'll give them a quick ending when they clear all but the last five bubbles in the top row. When that happens, the remaining top row bubbles will pop, and everything else will drop down as if it were an orphaned group (using the kaboom routine).

ANTICIPATE AND ALLEVIATE PLAYER FRUSTRATIONS

Always think ahead about how your game could become frustrating and solve the problem in advance. By doing so, you'll improve the game and keep players coming back for more. In *Bubble Shooter*, a level could be impossible to complete because the bubbles didn't appear in the correct order. This situation is a perfect example of what can happen when a possible outcome—in this case, a *single* bubble being left on the board and not being poppable—isn't considered during the original game design. Game programming is almost always iterative, and rarely will your first version be the final one.

After we calculate the current set to pop, we'll check how many bubbles are left anytime the player pops bubbles. If five or fewer bubbles remain on the board after the player has finished firing bubbles, we'll pop those for free and take the player straight to the game's end.

The check to determine if the level is nearly complete will be inside clickGameScreen in *game.js*:

game.js
```
var BubbleShoot = window.BubbleShoot || {};
  BubbleShoot.Game = (function($){
  var Game = function(){
    --snip--
    var clickGameScreen = function(e){
      --snip--
      if(collision){
        var coords = collision.coords;
        duration = Math.round(duration * collision.distToCollision /
          distance);
        board.addBubble(curBubble,coords);
        var group = board.getGroup(curBubble,{});
        if(group.list.length >= 3){
          popBubbles(group.list,duration);
❶        var topRow = board.getRows()[0];
❷        var topRowBubbles = [];
          for(var i=0;i<topRow.length;i++){
            if(topRow[i])
              topRowBubbles.push(topRow[i]);
          };
❸        if(topRowBubbles.length <= 5){
❹          popBubbles(topRowBubbles,duration);
❺          group.list.concat(topRowBubbles);
          };
```

```
                var orphans = board.findOrphans();
                var delay = duration + 200 + 30 * group.list.length;
                dropBubbles(orphans,delay);
❻              var popped = [].concat(group.list,orphans);
                var points = popped.length * POINTS_PER_BUBBLE;
                score += points;
                setTimeout(function(){
                  BubbleShoot.ui.drawScore(score);
                },delay);
              };
            }else{
              --snip--
            };
            --snip--
          };
          --snip--
        };
        return Game;
})(jQuery);
```

First, we retrieve the top row ❶, and then we loop through it, counting the number of bubbles ❷. If five or fewer bubbles are present ❸, we pop all of the bubbles in the top row ❹ and add them to the list of popped bubbles ❺ so they contribute to the player's score ❻.

You should now be able to play through an entire game level, clear the board, and see a prompt to start the next level. Congratulations! You just finished your first fully playable game.

But before you put *Bubble Shooter* in front of another player, let's make the high score persist from one session to the next rather than resetting every time the browser window is closed. After all, what's the point of a high score if you can't come back to challenge it later?

High Score Persistence with Web Storage

Although *Bubble Shooter* has no server-side component to save high scores, we can use the Web Storage system that comes with HTML5 to save them to the local machine. Players who play again with the same browser will see the previous high score, which gives them a target to beat.

Bubble Shooter is a casual game: the user will open it, play a few levels until they fail, and then close the browser tab. Remembering the high score is a good idea, but we don't need to retain any other data. Regardless, the principle of using Web Storage to persist data from one game session to the next is the same even if you're storing a much larger amount of information.

Web Storage vs. Cookies

On the client side, Web Storage behaves in a similar way to cookies, but the implementation details (and advantages) are very different. Web Storage is easier to access than cookies are because data is stored in name/value pairs. Unlike with cookies, there is no server-side access to the contents of

Web Storage, because data isn't transmitted as part of an HTTP request. The contents of the store are restricted by domain, so different subdomains have different stores. We could store the high score in a cookie, but there's no reason to do so, and the storage format as well as the overhead of transmitting data unnecessarily to the server on each request makes a cookie a worse option than Web Storage. Trying to store large amounts of data (such as the layout of the current board) in a cookie can also cause performance issues, because this data is transmitted to the server with each request. For example, when the browser tries to download an image file of only a few kilobytes, it could also have to send a large amount of extraneous data to the server.

Web Storage, on the other hand, gives you more space than cookies do, although the exact amount isn't defined in the HTML specification and is set individually by the browser vendors. The current lowest common figure among the main web browsers is 5MB; that limit applies to all data stored within a domain. Google Chrome, Firefox, and Internet Explorer 9 on a desktop all provide up to 10MB, but the Android browser on phone and tablet devices provides as little as 2MB. Compare that with the maximum cookie storage—anything upwards of 300 cookies of 4KB each—and you can see that even at the lower limits, Web Storage provides much more storage.

Because browser limits can change regularly, if you plan to place large amounts of data into Web Storage, there's no substitute for testing on specific devices; however, for small elements such as the high score in *Bubble Shooter*, the space limits are irrelevant.

Adding Data to Web Storage

Web Storage comes in two parts: Session Storage and Local Storage. We'll only look at Local Storage, which is best for persisting data across sessions. The principles of storing and accessing data are largely the same for Session Storage, although the persistence and security differ slightly. As the name might imply, Session Storage only persists for the duration of the browser session. The data disappears when the user closes their browser window. This type of storage might be useful for a multipage web application where data needs to persist from one page to the next, but it's obviously unsuited to storing a high score. Once you're familiar with Local Storage, you'll be able to adapt to working with Session Storage if you need to use it.

The format for adding a piece of data to `localStorage` is as follows:

```
localStorage.setItem(key,value);
```

The `key` is a string, such as `"high_score"`, and `value` is also a string, or a number or other object that can be automatically converted to a string. Note that if you try to pass in a complex object, such as an array, the conversion to a string may result in the name of the object (that is, `Array`) rather than the data you want to store. So if in doubt, perform a conversion yourself. For more complex data, you can use `JSON.stringify` to save objects and `JSON.parse` to retrieve them.

To retrieve data, you just need the key:

```
var value = localStorage.getItem(key);
```

`localStorage.getItem` always returns values as strings, so you'll need to use `parseInt` or `parseFloat` to convert them to numerical data.

If the game were more complex or took longer to play, you might want to save more data, such as the current level as well as the high score. In that case, we could just keep on adding strings:

```
localStorage.setItem("high_score",highScore);
localStorage.setItem("level",level);
```

Or we could create an object and JSON encode it:

```
var gameData = {high_score : highScore, level : level};
localStorage.setItem("bubbleshoot_data",JSON.stringify(gameData));
```

Then, when we want to retrieve the data, we would use this:

```
var gameData = JSON.parse(localStorage.getItem("bubbleshoot_data"));
```

The general principle is that if you can convert your data into a string and decode it from a string when you want to retrieve it, you can save it to Local Storage.

In *Bubble Shooter*, to save the high score, the Local Storage entry will be called `high_score`. At game initialization, we want to check whether an existing value is stored and, if so, use that in place of the zero that is currently hardcoded in. When the player has set a new record, we'll set the Local Storage value to the new high score.

In *game.js*, we'll make additions to `init` and `endGame` to retrieve and set the high score:

game.js
```
var BubbleShoot = window.BubbleShoot || {};
BubbleShoot.Game = (function($){
  var Game = function(){
    --snip--
    this.init = function(){
      if(BubbleShoot.Renderer){
        BubbleShoot.Renderer.init(function(){
          $(".but_start_game").click("click",startGame);
        });
      }else{
        $(".but_start_game").click("click",startGame);
      };
```

```
❶      if(window.localStorage && localStorage.getItem("high_score")){
❷        highScore = parseInt(localStorage.getItem("high_score"));
       }
❸      BubbleShoot.ui.drawHighScore(highScore);
     };
     --snip--
     var endGame = function(hasWon){
       if(score > highScore){
         highScore = score;
         $("#new_high_score").show();
         BubbleShoot.ui.drawHighScore(highScore);
❹        if(window.localStorage){
❺          localStorage.setItem("high_score",highScore);
         }
       }else{
         $("#new_high_score").hide();
       };
       if(hasWon){
         level++;
       }else{
         score = 0;
         level = 0;
       };
       $(".but_start_game").click("click",startGame);
       $("#board .bubble").remove();
       BubbleShoot.ui.endGame(hasWon,score);
     };
   };
   return Game;
})(jQuery);
```

First, we check whether localStorage is supported by the browser, by
using another Modernizr detector, and whether a value for high_score
exists ❶. If a high score exists, we set highScore to the contents in the store ❷.
We make sure to wrap the value with a parseInt, because values in the store
are returned as strings and we want to work with an integer. We then display
the high score ❸. To save the score, we add a line to endGame to check whether
localStorage is supported ❹ and then save to it ❺.

Reload the browser and play through a game. At first, any score you get
should become the new high score. But if you close the browser and reload
the game, the high score should be populated with your previous value.

You could also use Web Storage to save things like language prefer-
ences, player profiles, or game state progression. Just be mindful of what
you store there, because the values inside the storage system are open
to calls from the JavaScript console. That means there's nothing to stop
particularly tech-savvy players from updating data themselves! In the next
chapter, we'll briefly discuss security issues in HTML5 games, but for now
we can rely on the fact that there's really no incentive to set an impossibly
high score to try to beat.

Smoothing Animations with requestAnimationFrame

We use `setTimeout` to time animations in *jquery.kaboom.js* and when we trigger frame updates in the canvas version of *Bubble Shooter*. `setTimeout` is cross-browser compatible and relatively simple: set the timeout value to 40 milliseconds, and you can expect 25 frames per second.

However, there are downsides to using `setTimeout`. The main problem is that if the browser is busy with something else, the next iteration may not be called for more than 40 milliseconds. In some cases, it might take a lot longer and the user will start to notice.

We could recode movement so that objects move a distance proportional to the time elapsed since the last update, effectively ignoring the 40 millisecond figure. But we'd still have to accept the fact that whatever value we set the timeout delay to will be too low for some setups and those displays won't be able to keep up. On systems that can handle much faster updates, we could display much smoother animations, but if we set the timeout value to 10 milliseconds to handle those cases, slower systems will see an adverse effect.

Fortunately, HTML5 introduced `requestAnimationFrame`, an alternative to `setTimeout` that is better suited to animation. Rather than making the programmer guess what kind of frame rate *might* work, the browser calls the function passed to `requestAnimationFrame` whenever it is ready to draw a new update. The time between updates might be much faster (or slower!) than 40 milliseconds, but at least we know that we're neither making a processing logjam worse nor having the system sit idle when we could spend extra cycles smoothing the animations.

A New Perspective on Frame Updates

We have to think differently about frame updates when switching to `requestAnimationFrame`. Currently, *before* `setTimeout` runs, we tell the browser how long to wait. We assume that the time elapsed is the time we expected to elapse. For example, in `moveAll` in *jquery.kaboom.js*, we set a timeout of 40 milliseconds:

```
setTimeout(moveAll,40);
```

We then update the position of the bubbles assuming that 40 milliseconds—1/25th of a second—has elapsed. However, with `requestAnimationFrame`, we don't specify a frame rate. In the `moveAll` function in *jquery.kaboom.js*, if `requestAnimationFrame` did happen to run this routine every 40 milliseconds, we wouldn't need to change anything. But if it ran every, say, 20 milliseconds, we couldn't keep the same values of `dx` and `dy`, or our whole animation would run much faster—twice as fast, in fact, because it would add `dx` and `dy` twice as often.

Instead, we need to find out how many milliseconds have elapsed and then adjust our animation step size. We can even apply the same math techniques to `setTimeout` animations to get better results on older browsers that don't support requestAnimationFrame. As shown in Figure 7-3, the less time that's elapsed since the bubble was last drawn, the less distance we have to move it along its path.

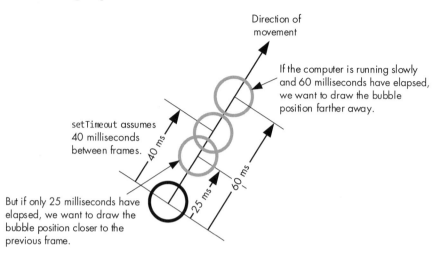

Figure 7-3: Bubble positions with different frame rates

Code Compatibility with Polyfills

Modernizr will help us build the setTimeout fallback. requestAnimationFrame is still regarded as prestandards by many browsers, so prefixed versions are available for Webkit, Mozilla, and so on, which Modernizr can fill in for us. Add the following to *game.js*:

game.js
```
var BubbleShoot = window.BubbleShoot || {};
  BubbleShoot.Game = (function($){
  var Game = function(){
    --snip--
  };
  window.requestAnimationFrame = Modernizr.prefixed("requestAnimationFrame",
    window) || function(callback){
    window.setTimeout(function(){
      callback();
    }, 40);
  };
  return Game;
})(jQuery);
```

This single line of new code says that if requestAnimationFrame (vendor-prefixed if necessary) is defined, then set window.requestAnimationFrame to the contents of requestAnimationFrame. If requestAnimationFrame is not defined, then we create a new function that accepts a function as a parameter and calls that function after 40 milliseconds using setTimeout.

This technique is known as a *polyfill*. Polyfills attempt to mimic or patch in new functionality to a browser where it's not supported natively, allowing you to use new technologies in your code without having to always worry about forking your code or providing fallbacks yourself. The name comes from the filling substance Polyfilla, because the technique involves filling in the cracks in browser support.

Polyfills are written to support all kinds of functionality in older browsers. For example, to store the player's high score, we're using the Local Storage API. This isn't available in older browsers, but we could achieve the same effect by storing the data in a cookie. There are two ways to approach this: one way is to write an if/else statement every time we access Local Storage to check if it exists and, if not, branch to run some cookie code. Alternatively, we could create an object called localStorage and add methods for getItem and setItem that use cookies to save and retrieve data.

Polyfills are rarely perfect solutions: setTimeout and requestAnimationFrame may operate in very similar ways, but sometimes the differences may be important. In the Local Storage example, we might be able to use cookies in exactly the same way as Local Storage, but if we tried to store a lot of data, we'd run into problems. Polyfills can enhance browser compatibility without a lot of code, but it's important to know the limitations of any polyfill you use.

Once we have the polyfill for requestAnimationFrame, as far as the rest of our code is concerned, requestAnimationFrame is supported, and we can use it regardless of the browser. We know that in truth, a setTimeout call is running behind the scenes and that sometimes the animation won't run as smoothly as it would with the natively supported requestAnimationFrame method. But as far as the code that calls it is concerned, the function behaves in the same way.

Now that we have a working requestAnimationFrame polyfill, we can replace our calls to setTimeout in *game.js* with calls to the new function in startGame and renderFrame:

game.js

```
var BubbleShoot = window.BubbleShoot || {};
  BubbleShoot.Game = (function($){
  var Game = function(){
    --snip--
    var startGame = function(){
      --snip--
      if(BubbleShoot.Renderer)
      {
        if(!requestAnimationID)
          requestAnimationID = requestAnimationFrame(renderFrame);
      }else{
        BubbleShoot.ui.drawBoard(board);
      };
      --snip--
    };
    --snip--
    var renderFrame = function(){
      $.each(bubbles,function(){
```

```
        if(this.getSprite().updateFrame)
            this.getSprite().updateFrame();
        });
        BubbleShoot.Renderer.render(bubbles,board.calculateTop());
        requestAnimationID = requestAnimationFrame(renderFrame);
    };
    --snip--
    };
    --snip--
    return Game;
})(jQuery);
```

We must make similar changes inside *jquery.kaboom.js* to use requestAnimationFrame rather than setTimeout. The kaboom function internally assumes that 40 milliseconds elapses between frames, giving a frame rate of 25 frames per second, but as we now know, with requestAnimationFrame the elapsed time may vary. Again, we need to calculate how much time has elapsed and calculate movement proportionally:

```
(function(jQuery){
    var defaults = {
        gravity : 1.3,
        maxY : 800
    };
    var toMove = [];
❶  var prevTime;
    var moveAll = function(){
❷      var newTime = Date.now();
❸      var elapsed = newTime - prevTime;
❹      var frameProportion = elapsed / 25;
❺      prevTime = newTime;
        var stillToMove = [];
        for(var i=0;i<toMove.length;i++){
            var obj = toMove[i];
            obj.x += obj.dx * frameProportion;
            obj.y -= obj.dy * frameProportion;
            obj.dy -= obj.config.gravity * frameProportion;
            if(obj.y < obj.config.maxY){
                obj.elm.css({
                    top : Math.round(obj.y),
                    left : Math.round(obj.x)
                });
                stillToMove.push(obj);
            }else if(obj.config.callback){
                obj.config.callback();
            }
        };
        toMove = stillToMove;
        if(toMove.length > 0)
❻          requestAnimationFrame(moveAll);
    };
    jQuery.fn.kaboom = function(settings)
```

```
    {
      var elm = this;
      var config = $.extend({}, defaults, settings);
      if(toMove.length == 0){
        prevTime = Date.now();
❼       requestAnimationFrame(moveAll);
      };
      var dx = Math.round(Math.random() * 10) - 5;
      var dy = Math.round(Math.random() * 5) + 5;
      toMove.push({
        elm : this,
        dx : dx,
        dy : dy,
        x : this.position().left,
        y : this.position().top,
        config : config
      });
    };
})(jQuery);
```

First, we define an empty variable called prevTime ❶ to store the timestamp of the last rendered frame, which is null initially. Each time moveAll is called, we retrieve the current timestamp ❷ and calculate the time elapsed since the last frame ❸. Our initial calculations were based on 40 milliseconds having elapsed, so to calculate the correct position, we scale the proportion of the frame elapsed accordingly ❹. If only 8 milliseconds have elapsed, frameProportion will be 0.2, and the animation will update in smaller but more frequent steps. If 80 milliseconds have elapsed, frameProportion will be 2, and the animation will update in larger steps. The end effect is that the bubbles take the same time to drop off the screen regardless of the frame rate. To prepare for the next frame, we update prevTime to the current timestamp ❺.

Also, setTimeout is replaced with requestAnimationFrame in two places: once when the animation is started ❻ and once for each frame loop ❼.

Reload the game and run it again to make sure it works properly. You probably won't see a difference in performance unless you have a particularly slow browser setup. However, now you can be confident that everyone who plays *Bubble Shooter* will see bubbles moving and falling at the same speeds, even if the frame update rates vary between devices.

Adding Sound with HTML5

A game never feels like a game without sound! HTML5 provides some increasingly powerful options for processing and playing back audio. I say *increasingly powerful* because browser support is being improved all the time. You can manipulate wave files byte by byte, record from the microphone, perform dynamic mixing, and take advantage of a whole host of features in addition to the woeful audio options that HTML offered not long ago. Let's look at the basic features of HTML5 audio.

The HTML5 Audio API

Historically, HTML has implemented audio poorly, offering no reliable way to embed and control sounds within web pages. This changed with HTML5, and you can embed a sound directly into a page with a simple tag, such as this one:

```
<audio src="sounds.mp3" autoplay></autoplay>
```

On its own, this isn't a lot of help for a game in which we want to programmatically start and stop sounds so they can react to events like bubbles popping. Fortunately, HTML5 also provides a way to play audio through a JavaScript API without using HTML tags at all.

The JavaScript equivalent of the preceding HTML fragment, which just embeds and plays a single file, is this:

```
var sound = new Audio("sounds.mp3");
sound.play();
```

You can try this with any MP3 file you have. The parameter passed into the new Audio call is the URL to the sound file. If you place it in the *bubbleshoot* folder and change the parameter to the file's name, you can run the previous command in the JavaScript console and the sound should play.

The sound will stop naturally when it ends, and you can use the stop method to end a sound at any point during playback:

```
sound.stop()
```

Those are the only commands we need, but take time to look through the audio API specification to see the growing potential for sound delivery in browsers. As well as methods and properties that affect the basic playback of audio, such as changing the volume of a sound or skipping to a specific point in a file, there is functionality for recording from input devices, mixing sounds, changing stereo, and even 3D sound positioning, as well as ways to post-process sounds to add effects such as echo. These are increasingly being supported in mainstream browsers, such as Google Chrome and Firefox, with improvements arriving in each new version.

If you want to play multiple sounds simultaneously, you must create multiple Audio objects. For example:

```
var sound1 = new Audio("sounds.mp3");
var sound2 = new Audio("sounds.mp3");
sound1.play();
sound2.play();
```

To just play different sounds one after another, you could reuse an Audio object by changing the object's src property. But to play multiple sounds at the same time, you need as many objects in existence as sounds that you plan to play simultaneously. As you'll see in *Bubble Shooter*, this means that if we want to pop a group of 20 bubbles, we'll need 20 sound objects to play the 20 popping sounds at the same time.

Popping Bubbles: Complete with Sound

We'll add HTML5 sound support to *Bubble Shooter* using the audio API so a sound plays for each bubble popped. Grab the file *pop.mp3* from *http://www.buildanhtml5game.com/* and put it in a new folder called *_mp3* inside the game folder.

First, create a class to play the sounds. We'll wrap the HTML5 audio functionality in our own code, which will prevent an error from being thrown in browsers that don't support HTML5 audio. Create a new file in the *_js* folder called *sounds.js* and then add the file to load in *index.html*. Sound processing, like rendering and the user interface, is another piece of functionality that's best to keep separate from game logic wherever possible. By creating a separate file to handle playback, we can put all of our sound-handling code in one place.

We'll reuse Audio objects, so we'll create these as the code is initialized. Then, whenever a sound needs to play, we'll pull out the next object in the queue, change the src to the file we want to play, and then play it. We'll set a cap of 10 sounds that can play simultaneously, which is a low number, but even on the rare occasion when a player is popping more than 10 bubbles at a time, there's no need to play more than 10 sounds.

sounds.js

```
var BubbleShoot = window.BubbleShoot || {};
BubbleShoot.Sounds = (function(){
❶   var soundObjects = [];
❷   for(var i=0;i<10;i++){
       soundObjects.push(new Audio());
     }
❸   var curSoundNum = 0;
❹   var Sounds = {
❺     play : function(url,volume){
         if(Modernizr.audio){
❻           var sound = soundObjects[curSoundNum];
❼           sound.src = url;
❽           sound.volume = volume;
❾           sound.play();
❿           curSoundNum++
           if(curSoundNum >= soundObjects.length){
             curSoundNum = curSoundNum % soundObjects.length;
           }
         }
       }
     }
   };
   return Sounds;
})();
```

A new object called `BubbleShoot.Sounds` contains the array `soundObjects` ❶, which we'll use to store the ten `Audio` objects. These are initialized as soon as the code is loaded ❷. We also keep track of which object to use with the variable `curSoundNum` ❸.

Next, we create the object to play the sound ❹, which contains a single method to play a sound ❺. It will accept two parameters: the URL of the sound file to play and the volume to play the sound at, which is a decimal number between 0 (silent) and 1 (full volume).

We use Modernizr to check whether or not HTML5 audio is supported, and if it is, we grab the current `Audio` object from the `soundObjects` array ❻, set its `src` property to the URL of the file to play ❼, set its volume ❽, and then play it ❾. If audio isn't supported, the method will do nothing, but because of our check for `Modernizr.audio`, no error will be thrown.

Finally, we increment the value of `curSoundNum` ❿ so that next time play is called, we will grab the next object in the queue. Then, we make sure that the value of `curSoundNum` is never greater than the number of `sound` objects in the `soundObjects` array.

If we want to play more sounds, we could push more `Audio` objects into the `soundObjects` array. Currently, if we try to play more than 10 sounds at once, only the last 10 sounds will play.

Sound control will happen inside *game.js* with a call to the `BubbleShoot.Sounds.play` function:

game.js

```
var BubbleShoot = window.BubbleShoot || {};
BubbleShoot.Game = (function($){
  var popBubbles = function(bubbles,delay){
    $.each(bubbles,function(){
      var bubble = this;
      setTimeout(function(){
        bubble.setState(BubbleShoot.BubbleState.POPPING);
        bubble.animatePop();
        setTimeout(function(){
          bubble.setState(BubbleShoot.BubbleState.POPPED);
        },200);
❶      BubbleShoot.Sounds.play("_mp3/pop.mp3"❷,Math.random()*.5 + .5❸);
      },delay);
      board.popBubbleAt(bubble.getRow(),bubble.getCol());
      setTimeout(function(){
        bubble.getSprite().remove();
      },delay + 200);
      delay += 60;
    });
  };
  --snip--
};
--snip--
return Game;
})(jQuery);
```

We want to play as many sounds as there are bubbles to pop, and we also want to start the sound at the same time we start the animation ❶. We pass the play method of Sounds two parameters: a relative URL to the MP3 file to play ❷ and a volume, which will be a random number between .5 and 1 ❸.

INCREASE IMMERSION WITH VARIETY

Why do we pass a random volume level? Try passing in a value of 1 and popping some bubbles. Then compare this effect to that of the random value. It's only a small change, but the variation in volume provides just enough differentiation between each sound to make it slightly less mechanical. We could do other things to make the effect even more natural, such as using a set of sounds rather than just one MP3 file so not every bubble sounds the same or changing the timing between pops so they aren't evenly spaced. Experimenting to create the most immersive experience possible and doing it with minimum effort are tasks you'll become more proficient at as you develop more games.

Summary

Now that we have a simple sound to add a bit of atmosphere, you've finished building *Bubble Shooter*! The game should play on older browsers, using CSS for positioning and animations, and it will work well on newer browsers that support the canvas element. We have persistent high scores and audio, and we've developed the animations in such a way that they should perform well regardless of the player's system speed.

In the next chapter, we'll explore some other parts of HTML5 that aren't directly related to the game you just built. You'll learn some pointers on how to deploy your game to Web and mobile environments, and you'll see what the future holds for HTML5.

Further Practice

1. Toward the end of each level, the player can only have bubbles of one, two, or three colors left on the board. Giving them a bubble of a color that won't match any of these causes the player to waste a shot and can make the game more difficult to complete. Change the bubble-generating algorithm so that it gives players only bubbles of a color that can potentially form a match. For example, if only red and blue bubbles remain, the firing bubble should be either red or blue. You will need to amend getNextBubble in *game.js* and choose a bubble type from one of the types that exist in the Board object.

2. As noted in "Multiple Levels and High Scores" on page 138, the game will become unplayable after a few levels because the number of bubbles allowed becomes too small. Instead of subtracting five bubbles per level, create an algorithm that makes levels progressively harder but makes it possible to complete a level. Perhaps the smallest number of fired bubbles a player can complete a level in is 30, and we want them to reach this level of difficulty on level 15. Before this point, the step from level 1 to 2 might be, say, five bubbles fewer, but the step from level 14 to 15 might be only one fewer. Write an equation or other method to decrease the number of bubbles allowed and increase the difficulty in this way.

3. Give players an incentive to repeat levels by awarding stars for a completion grade instead of the pass or fail condition that currently exists. You could award one star whenever the player clears the level, two stars if they clear with more than 25 percent of the level's bubble allocation remaining, and three stars if they complete the level by firing only half the bubbles they were given. Add information to the level completion dialog to show the player how many stars they earned.

4. Once you've added the preceding star system, create a way to store the number of stars the player has obtained for each level. Then you can show them not only how many stars they've attained but also a message when they beat a previous best. Currently, we store the number of bubbles remaining, the player's score, and current level number as variables inside Game. But now the best approach might be to create an object that stores each level and records the number of stars. Save this data to Local Storage for when the player returns to the game.

5. Write a polyfill to add Local Storage support to older browsers using cookies. You'll need to create an object called window.localStorage, if one doesn't already exist, and create getItem and setItem methods.

NEXT STEPS IN HTML5

In addition to graphical advances, HTML5 has a host of other features that make it a powerful game development environment. In this chapter, I'll discuss a few of them so you're aware of what features are available, and I'll point you to some useful resources for further reading.

Some of these features, such as WebGL, are subjects worthy of their own books, whereas others will be useful only for certain types of games. For these reasons, I'll only introduce the concepts here and leave more thorough exploration up to you.

Saving and Retrieving Data

People play games like *Bubble Shooter* in short sessions with little or no persistent data; in fact, our game saves only the high score from one session to the next. At present, the high score is stored in Web Storage, so it's unique to the browser the game is played on. To save a global high score and display a high score table, we'd need to write a server-side component that sends the score to a server and retrieves a list of high scores.

Games with more complex states should have server-side access, too. When you store state on the server, players can return to the same game from multiple devices. For our purposes, we'll use two main ways to save and retrieve data on a server: AJAX and WebSockets.

AJAX

AJAX (Asynchronous JavaScript and XML) provides a technique for sending a request to a server and receiving a response. AJAX is not a single technology but rather a method by which a number of tried-and-tested browser features are combined to make server-side calls and manage the responses. All of the major browsers have supported AJAX for a number of years.

Although the *X* stands for XML, you can use AJAX to retrieve HTML data, string data, and JSON strings that can be parsed and interpreted. The code for making AJAX calls is well documented, and multiple libraries are available so you don't have to handcraft the calls. For example, here's how you'd send an AJAX request to a server with the $.ajax call in jQuery:

```
$.ajax({
❶   url : "save_data.php",
❷   data : "high_score =" + highScore,
❸   type : "POST",
❹   complete : function(data){
      console.log(data);
    }
});
```

This $.ajax call makes a POST request to the relative URL *save_data.php*, sends the value contained in highScore to the server under the name high_score, and logs the server's response to the console. I set the URL target for the request ❶, the data to send ❷, the type of request ❸, and a function to run after the request completes ❹, but you can set many other properties, including functions to run in case of an error, timeout settings, and so on. These are listed in the jQuery documentation at *http://api.jquery.com/*.

NOTE   *The* A *in AJAX stands for* asynchronous, *because other JavaScript operations will continue while the server deals with the data and sends the response. That means you can't be sure when the* complete *function will run: it'll happen whenever the response comes back, but the user interface will remain responsive while it happens. It's possible to make synchronous calls, but because this effectively freezes the entire page until the request is complete, the user experience is generally so poor that doing so is considered bad practice.*

WebSockets

Most modern browsers also have WebSockets available to make client to server calls. WebSockets are a relatively new technology incorporated into the HTML5 specification. If you want to learn how they work at a lower level than I describe here, a good place to start is with the Mozilla Developer Network documentation at *https://developer.mozilla.org/en/docs/WebSockets/*.

WebSockets are similar to AJAX, but whereas AJAX sets up a call-and-response relationship between the client and server, a WebSocket maintains a persistent connection between them. The client deals with responses as they come in, and the JavaScript code can listen continuously for further responses. The server also constantly listens while the socket is open; therefore, WebSockets are much better than AJAX when conversations between the client and server involve lots of small data transactions.

A persistent connection is especially useful in multiplayer gaming environments. Before WebSockets, the main way to update game state elements shared by multiple clients, such as player avatars within an environment, was to continuously poll the server with AJAX and check for updates. This would be coded to happen every few seconds, which obviously isn't sufficient for a real-time game. People tried various hacks—such as a technique called *long-polling*, which effectively tricks the client into maintaining a connection to the server—to improve the process, but these were often inefficient in terms of server resources. Now, you can just leave a WebSocket open, and whenever one client updates the game state, the server can immediately update all of the other clients' information without waiting for the next update cycle.

Mainstream browsers have ever-improving support for WebSockets, and as with AJAX, I recommend using a library to eliminate some of the nitty-gritty of opening connections, sending and listening for data, and handling errors. Libraries will also often have a fallback to AJAX or other server communication methods for cases in which WebSockets aren't supported; however, the fallbacks may not replicate the performance features that you're using WebSockets for in the first place, so be aware that they're not a magic solution.

Socket.IO (*http://socket.io/*) is one of the most popular WebSocket libraries. Here's how you can use it to make a call:

```
var socket = io.connect("http://localhost");
  socket.emit("new_high_score", {
    high_score : highScore
  });
});
```

This code uses a call to the library with `io.connect` to open a new WebSocket and then `socket.emit` sends the `highScore` value as an event named `new_high_score`.

WebSockets and libraries such as Socket.IO have much greater capabilities than AJAX, but the libraries that make them easy to use often assume a specific server-side environment. If you plan to use WebSockets, check that the library you plan to use has a backend component that matches your server environment. Libraries for most platforms are readily available, whether you're using Node.js, .NET, or Java.

Along with sending and receiving data to and from the server, you might also want to process certain data outside your main game program. That's where Web Workers will come in handy.

Web Workers

JavaScript in a browser is generally considered a *single-threaded* environment, meaning that only one script can run at a time. This won't cause problems most of the time but can be an issue if a particularly large computational process blocks the processor from animating, responding to user input, and performing other important tasks.

For example, let's say processing game-level data takes the browser 1 or 2 seconds, and this happens every 30 seconds or so. The overall load may not be high, but you can't pause the game every 30 seconds! In this situation, consider using a Web Worker.

Web Workers (*https://developer.mozilla.org/en/docs/Web/API/Worker/*) allow you to run code in a separate thread without blocking your main JavaScript operations. They're called "workers" because you can essentially hand them a task and tell them to report back when they're finished. The browser will determine how much CPU time to give them so as not to interfere unduly with other processes. Workers can be dedicated or shared, but you'll generally find dedicated workers most useful, especially while support for Web Workers is being developed across browsers.

Web Workers follow a couple of rules that differentiate them from regular JavaScript. Most important, they have no access to the DOM, the browser document, or the browser window. Workers also operate within their own scope, so you'll need to pass data explicitly and then retrieve the result when complete. I'll illustrate how they work with the following example.

Workers are initialized by passing the name of a script to load to the new `Worker` command:

```
var worker = new Worker("work.js");
```

This will start a new worker, and that worker will run the script inside *work.js*.

A worker runs when you send it a message via `postMessage`:

```
worker.postMessage();
```

The `postMessage` command can contain a JavaScript object or be empty.

You can handle responses—values a worker returns when it completes a task—by adding event listeners to the worker within the calling script:

```
worker.addEventListener("message", function(e) {
  console.log(e.data);
}, false);
```

Here, e contains the data that worker sent back. The event to listen to, labeled "message", is any valid string. Therefore, a worker could send back different responses in different circumstances, or it could just keep working and sending messages.

Inside the worker, the model of event listeners is similar, with the worker referring to itself as this or self. As an example, *work.js* could contain the following to return the message:

```
self.addEventListener("message", function(e) {
  self.postMessage({
    message : "I'm done now"
  });
}, false);
```

This code listens for an event marked "message", and on receipt, it immediately posts a response in the form of an object.

At present, not all the major browsers support Web Workers well enough to make it reliable. Polyfills do exist for Web Workers, but these will often negatively affect your user's experience if a long-running process that you assumed would be nonblocking suddenly freezes the game for a few seconds. However, the situation is constantly improving, and hopefully, Web Workers will soon be considered a core part of the HTML5 game developer's arsenal.

But managing your data more effectively is just a start to making your game more fun. Appearance matters, too, and for a graphics upgrade, you can go 3D with WebGL or even use it to beef up your rendering power for 2D games.

WebGL

For the canvas version of *Bubble Shooter*, we used the 2D rendering context, accessed with calls along the lines of

```
var context = canvas.getContext("2d");
```

As I touched upon in Chapter 6, the specification of "2d" implies that other options are available, and sometimes, depending on browser support, that's true. The third dimension is accessed through WebGL, an API that provides a set of 3D manipulation functions for creating scenes, adding lighting and textures, positioning cameras, and so on, taking advantage of the acceleration that modern graphics cards provide. (Visit *https://www.khronos .org/registry/webgl/specs/1.0/* to learn about WebGL in more detail.) To start using WebGL, we first instantiate a 3D context with the following:

```
var context = canvas.getContext("webgl");
```

This is sometimes retrieved as `"experimental-webgl"`, so the most compatible call is this:

```
var context = canvas.getContext("webgl")
  || canvas.getContext("experimental-webgl");
```

Accelerated WebGL is powerful enough to display fully rendered 3D scenes rivaling those of native games. The downside is that working in three dimensions and manipulating and creating scenes requires a lot of math and a lot of low-level code that involves writing programs directly to the graphics processor. The concepts are the same as when creating 3D games in native code, such as C++, and require low-level knowledge of 3D modeling to describe the shape of an object; textures to define surface patterns; and shaders, which describe how to render a surface when light hits it. As such, I highly recommend working with existing libraries to handle model rendering, any physics requirements, and basically any features you can get off the shelf. Babylon.js (*http://www.babylonjs.com/*) and PlayCanvas (*https:// playcanvas.com/*) are two libraries that make working with WebGL in the browser much simpler.

Using WebGL also brings up the question of how to import objects and textures into 3D scenes. Typically, you create models in modeling software, such as 3D Studio or Maya, and then export to a commonly supported format. WebGL libraries generally won't work with those formats, so you'll usually need to convert from the original 3D modeling file format to JSON using another set of tools, such as the 3DS Max-to-Babylon.js exporter (*https://github.com/BabylonJS/Babylon.js/tree/master/Exporters/3ds%20Max*), which exports from Autodesk's 3D Studio product into Babylon.js.

Creating and converting 3D models is a large enough task that WebGL game development quickly becomes a project for teams of developers and designers rather than for a sole developer; however, many very impressive demos have been made entirely solo, and the Babylon.js website has a great set of showcases.

A secondary advantage of the WebGL context is that you can use it to render 2D scenes, which can then take advantage of the huge speed available through GPU acceleration. Particle effects and rendering large numbers of onscreen elements in accelerated WebGL far outperform the same tasks in the canvas.

I recommend that you look for off-the-shelf libraries that enable 2D rendering in WebGL. One such library is Pixi.js (*http://www.pixijs.com/*), which also provides a fallback to the canvas.

Browser support for WebGL is growing and includes the latest versions of Chrome, Firefox, and Internet Explorer, although older versions of Internet Explorer are incompatible at the time of this writing. For this reason, WebGL isn't considered ready for mass-market development, but this situation continues to improve.

Building a slick game is all well and good, but a game is nothing without players. To reach players, you need to deploy your game somewhere publicly accessible. Depending on where you deploy, you should consider some changes to improve the player's experience.

Deploying HTML5 Games

In this section, I'll give a brief overview of the process behind deploying a game running inside desktop and mobile browsers, and I'll explain how you'd wrap up an HTML5 application as a native mobile application.

Running Fullscreen in a Desktop Browser

One way to deploy an HTML5 game is to just create a website and upload it. In fact, just upload *Bubble Shooter* to the Web to make it accessible to anyone who accesses the *index.html* file. Deploying an HTML5 game to the Web is no different from deploying any other website; however, players often complain about a lack of immersion when they are running games in a browser, because it's easy to become distracted by tabs showing notifications from Facebook, email, instant messages, and so on. The HTML5 arsenal has a trick to fix these interruptions: the Fullscreen API.

Where supported, the Fullscreen API lets a web page fill the entire width and height of the screen, removing the address bar and other browser frame elements. You can implement fullscreen capabilities by running the following JavaScript code. For security reasons, you need to run this code inside a user-generated event handler; that is, you will usually make a button for the player to click or specify a key for them to press to activate fullscreen mode.

```
if(document.body.requestFullScreen) {
  document.body.requestFullScreen();
} else if(document.body.mozRequestFullScreen) {
  document.body.mozRequestFullScreen();
} else if(document.body.webkitRequestFullScreen) {
  document.body.webkitRequestFullScreen();
} else if(document.body.msRequestFullScreen){
  document.body.msRequestFullScreen();
}
```

Note the use of vendor prefixes while the requestFullScreen API is being implemented (mozRequestFullScreen for Firefox, webkitRequestFullScreen for Chrome, and so on). When you call requestFullScreen, the user should see a dialog from the browser asking whether to allow or deny your game's request to go fullscreen. If the player allows fullscreen, pressing the ESC key should return them to the regular view.

You can also apply fullscreen mode to a single element inside the DOM. You might want to do this if you have a game running within a website with navigation to other pages, for example. Then, players can go into fullscreen mode to remove the distractions of navigation bars and other page clutter. You could even apply fullscreen mode to *Bubble Shooter*. Just add a new tool-bar button that runs the following code when a player clicks the button:

```
if(document.body.requestFullScreen) {
  $("#page").get(0).requestFullScreen();
}else if(document.body.mozRequestFullScreen) {
  $("#page").get(0).mozRequestFullScreen();
}else if(document.body.webkitRequestFullScreen) {
  $("#page").get(0).webkitRequestFullScreen();
}else if(document.body.msRequestFullScreen){
  $("#page").get(0).msRequestFullScreen();
}
```

I'll leave this as an exercise for you to implement, and I suggest you add it to *ui.js* to keep it with the other user interface code. But if you'd rather not deploy to your own website, try a hosting service. You could set up an application on Facebook or upload a game to a dedicated game website, such as Kongregate.

Of course, the promise of cross-platform development and deployment is one of the biggest attractions of HTML5, and because most desktop browser features have been ported to mobile browsers, *Bubble Shooter* should work just as well on both. However, the behaviors aren't quite identical between platforms, and I'll discuss those differences next.

Running in a Mobile Browser

Even if you're still running *Bubble Shooter* on a local or development web server, you should be able to load the game in a mobile browser and play it. It should function just as well as it does on a desktop browser. Congratulations, you've just made your first mobile game!

NOTE   *In case you haven't deployed the game yet, you can also play it at* http://buildanhtml5game.com/bubbleshooter/.

When developing games for mobile devices, it's more likely you'll need to make usability and interface changes than technical ones, but that's not to say you can ignore implementation changes completely. You'll benefit from knowing the subtle differences in behavior and how to optimize the experience for mobile users, so let's get started.

Touch Events

First, touchscreen-specific events are implemented by browsers on touch-screen devices. Two of those events are touchstart and touchend, which are roughly equivalent to mousedown and mouseup, respectively. However, the click event differs slightly in a touchscreen environment. Mobile browsers wait a few hundred milliseconds to determine whether the user double-taps, which is a zoom operation, to make absolutely sure that the user intends a single click. This won't make much difference in *Bubble Shooter*, but for rapid-reaction games, those few hundred milliseconds will be noticeable to the player.

You can use mobile-specific events, and they'll be ignored on desktop devices without a touchscreen, although for the most part, using mousedown will have the same effect as touchstart and mouseup will be equivalent to touchend. For example, in *Bubble Shooter*, we could use mousedown instead of click to detect when the player wants to fire a bubble, which would turn this line from *game.js*:

```
$("#game").bind("click",clickGameScreen);
```

into this line of code instead:

```
$("#game").bind("mousedown",clickGameScreen);
```

The only effect would be that the bubble will fire when the user clicks the mouse button down or touches the screen rather than waiting for the mouse button to be released or the finger removed from the screen.

NOTE *Using only the mouse and touch events will remove keyboard accessibility if you have a game that could conceivably be controlled by the keyboard. In some games, you might want to continue using the click event so a player could still, for example, navigate a menu system using the keyboard or other input device.*

If you know that your game will be played only on a mobile device, you could also use touchstart:

```
$("#game").bind("touchstart",clickGameScreen);
```

This should work the same way as mousedown.

You may be wondering, then, why touchstart and touchend exist at all if they're virtually equivalent to mousedown and mouseup. The answer is that in most cases you can treat them as conceptually equivalent, but touch events can be useful if you want to detect more than one touch point simultane-ously. The user will (usually) have only one mouse pointer, but it's possible to make contact with a touchscreen in multiple places. If you're building a game that requires this kind of input, touch events are the ones to use, and you'll have to find a way to make them work in a mouse environment.

Scaling

Another interaction difference comes into play with zooming. You probably don't want players zooming into the game area at all, whether they double-tap or not. Fortunately, you can restrict this by adding <meta> tags to the HTML head:

```
<meta name="viewport" content="user-scalable=no, initial-scale=1,
maximum-scale=1, minimum-scale=1, width=device-width, height=device-height" />
```

This example tells the browser to render the page at a scale of 1:1 and set the viewport width to the default for the device. The content of the <meta> tag specifies the size of the display and restricts (or allows) zooming. Apple originally introduced this <meta> tag, and other browsers use it as a basis for their own behavior. Hence, Apple's own documentation (*https://developer.apple.com/library/ios/documentation/AppleApplications/Reference/SafariWebContent/UsingtheViewport/UsingtheViewport.html*) is the best place to look for a description of the various options. However, using this tag is very much a case of looking up what's expected to happen in any particular mobile browser and then testing it to see how it works in practice. Work is underway to standardize viewport sizing using CSS (*http://www.w3.org/TR/css-device-adapt/*), although it has minimal browser support at present.

The most common option you'll use in the <meta> tag is user-scalable=no, which simply prevents the user from zooming. But changing the other values in the <meta> tag can greatly affect how the browser displays your game, too. The settings in the <meta> tag are as follows:

user-scalable   Can be yes or no. Allows or disables zooming.

initial-scale   A decimal number specifying the zoom factor at which to draw the viewport.

maximum-scale   A decimal representing the maximum zoomable scale to allow the user to zoom to.

minimum-scale   A decimal representing the minimum zoomable scale to allow the user to zoom to.

width   Specify this in pixels, or use device-width.

height   Specify this in pixels, or use device-height.

If the game is designed with a width of, say, 760 pixels, you could set width to 760, and the browser would keep the page at that width and eliminate any extra pixels of spacing on either side. Unfortunately, by scaling the viewport, you'll almost certainly have to solve problems with image scaling and aspect ratio; trying to draw 760 pixels on a screen that's made up of 1024 pixels means some aliasing will need to occur.

Aspect ratios also vary much more between mobile devices than desktop screens. For example, the iPad 1 and 2 have a resolution of 1024×768, the iPad 3 is 2048×1536, the iPhone 6 is 750×1334, the iPhone 6 Plus is 1080×1920, and there are almost as many Android resolutions as there are devices. Unfortunately, no simple solution exists. Be sure to test continually on a wide range of devices, and experiment with a combination of <meta> properties and CSS layouts to ensure your game looks good on a variety of screen sizes and aspect ratios.

Of course, even after you solve the aspect ratio problem, if users are still playing your game through a mobile browser, they may not be able to play while offline. To really get an HTML5 game onto the device, you need to wrap up the code in a native package. When your game is a native application, the user should be able to play it whether online or offline, unless your game requires an Internet connection anyway. Let's look at using a wrapper service next.

Deploying as a Native Application

You have two main ways to deploy your HTML5 game as a native web application. You can write a wrapper using Objective-C, Java, or whichever language the target platform requires, or you can use an existing wrapper service. Unless you're very proficient with native mobile coding, I highly recommend that you look at a wrapper service.

Wrapper services, such as PhoneGap/Cordova (*http://cordova.apache.org/*) and Ludei (*https://www.ludei.com/*), give you less control, but they often provide access to native features, such as accelerometers and in-app purchases. Sometimes they even offer accelerated graphics capabilities and bespoke APIs. They require less time and effort, too, making them an excellent way to build test deployments so you can quickly see your game running on a device. I'd advise using a service unless you have a very good reason not to.

Using a third-party wrapper often involves uploading your HTML5 code through an online service and downloading a compiled version for each device. These services effectively do the same work as custom wrappers, but they've been optimized over iterations, usually for multiple platforms. They also continue to add support for newer handsets and operating systems, which is very time consuming to keep on top of yourself. In addition, a community is usually writing plug-ins to provide extra functionality, such as offering in-app purchases or accessing the device's camera.

Just remember that no matter how you decide to wrap your HTML5 application, the files will all be running in a local environment; that is, your game won't need to download assets over the Web or from a server. As a result, your game will be playable even when no web connection is available. If you're developing a multiplayer game, it will need an Internet connection to be active, but even then your game will benefit from faster startup times and (if your game is a hit) it will save on bandwidth costs. As always, perform constant iterative testing to intercept problems before they become major issues.

That's the end of my mobile tour, but on a desktop browser, *Bubble Shooter* is simple enough that unless you're playing on a very low-powered machine, you shouldn't run into performance problems. But at some point, as you develop more complex games, you'll find that some piece of code runs slower than intended, and then you'll want to optimize that code.

Optimization

Two main areas to look at when you're optimizing a game are memory management and speed. In particular, you should ensure your game doesn't consume increasing amounts of system resources the longer it runs, and you'll want to make the most of available hardware and coding tricks for speed.

Whether or not you encounter visible problems, such as slowing animation, continually checking your game's performance is good practice. You'll likely only need to optimize for speed as a result of a specific problem, but keeping an eye on memory utilization is good practice in all cases. For example, a game may run fine when you play for five minutes, but if you leave it open in a browser tab for hours on end, you may return to find your nice animation loop eating up tens or hundreds of megabytes of memory because of a leak. For less powerful mobile devices, this can be a real problem.

Fortunately, browser tools can help identify and diagnose problems, and you can implement coding techniques to fix those problems or minimize the risk of them happening. Good memory management is particularly important, so we'll look at that before we move on to speed optimization.

Memory Management

You might not expect a small JavaScript game to run into memory issues on systems that happily run massive 3D games, but memory management is actually a pressing concern for HTML5 game developers. The problem is less about running out of memory (although it is possible, with some effort, to use up a vast amount of memory) and more about the way JavaScript allocates memory and frees it up later. Rather than constantly allocating and freeing memory, browsers run through periodic sweeps to clear memory, which can cause jittery animations, unresponsive interfaces, and general interruption of game flow.

Writing JavaScript in ways that minimize memory usage is a large subject, and browser vendors often publish papers on how to get the best out of their systems. For example, check out Mozilla's documentation on memory management at *https://developer.mozilla.org/en-US/docs/Web/JavaScript/Memory_Management/*. You can also read an excellent introduction to memory-efficient JavaScript, written by one of the Chrome engineers, Addy Osmani, at *http://www.smashingmagazine.com/2012/11/05/writing-fast-memory-efficient-javascript/*.

The key to dealing with memory issues is identifying them in the first place. You may suspect you have a problem, but you need to know where it is. The main desktop browsers have tools to help. Those tools are constantly evolving, so I won't discuss them in depth. But a search through the documentation for each browser should bring up relevant documents and tutorials, such as the one for Chrome at *https://developer.chrome.com/devtools/docs/javascript-memory-profiling/*.

Here's where to start in the three major browsers:

- In Chrome, open Developer Tools and click **Profiles**. Select **Take Heap Snapshot** and click **Take Snapshot** to examine objects in memory, including DOM elements. Figure 8-1 shows how this looks for *Bubble Shooter*.

- In Firefox, you can use Firebug and other plug-ins to examine objects in memory. You can also type `about:memory` into the address bar for a snapshot of what's currently in the browser's memory..

- In Internet Explorer 11, open the Developer Tools and select the **Memory** tool.

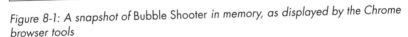

Figure 8-1: A snapshot of Bubble Shooter *in memory, as displayed by the Chrome browser tools*

Another useful tool is to visualize when garbage collection is occurring. This takes the form of a graph across time, and you can see what range of memory your game is occupying. Figure 8-2 shows *Bubble Shooter*'s memory usage over time.

The sawtooth line represents memory used when objects are created. The line rises, and then it sharply drops when garbage collection occurs. Although we're not creating and destroying many objects, there's a definite sign that if we saw problems with animations not running smoothly, we could look at using more object pools.

The key to maintaining fast animations is to test and iterate. This is especially true when developing for mobile devices, where debugging tools are usually slightly harder to access and where memory and processing power are also usually less abundant. If you notice intermittent slowdowns and animation freezes that are difficult to reproduce, it's likely that you have a memory issue to identify and address.

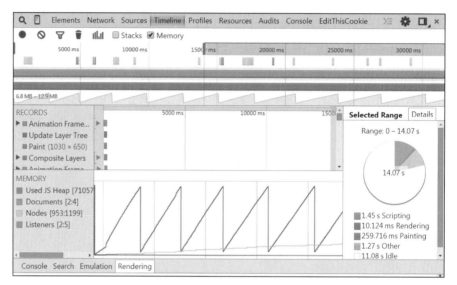

Figure 8-2: Memory usage by Bubble Shooter

Optimizing for Speed

Memory may or may not be an issue, depending on your game's needs, and memory fixes occasionally require coding techniques somewhat at odds with writing readable, reusable code. However, optimizing for speed is more achievable as a side effect of following general best practices.

JavaScript engines are improving in speed all the time and so are browsers' rendering engines (especially with the addition of WebGL). But, as with garbage collection, you should still be aware of the pain points. The browser vendors won't solve all your performance problems for you. In reality, JavaScript interpreters are becoming so fast that speed problems are more likely to occur while rendering than anywhere else; however, coding techniques can make the translation between JavaScript and machine code more efficient and speed up operations, such as passing image data to the rendering engine.

Each time you add or change an element in the DOM, the browser has to work out what to draw and where to draw it. HTML documents were originally designed as flowing, text-based documents, and the browser will assume the content you send it is meant to be laid out like any other web page.

But actions that cause the browser to repaint the display, such as adding new elements to the screen or changing an element's coordinates, are very common in games. In *Bubble Shooter*, we can get away with adding and removing elements as we want because relatively few elements are onscreen. Multiply the number of items onscreen by 10 or 100, and you'll start to see problems. Remember that the garbage collector needs to sweep away any element deleted from the scene, and DOM elements tend to be complex.

By contrast, the canvas copes with graphical additions without an expensive paint operation because no reflowing occurs inside a canvas element. The browser considers canvas elements to be images, which are just streams of pixels that go from memory to screen.

NOTE   *Changing properties of the canvas element, such as its position or transparency, rather than pixels within it, is just as expensive as changing any other DOM element.*

You can see how much time the browser spends painting a scene by loading *Bubble Shooter* in the Chrome desktop browser, pressing F12 to open Developer Tools, and navigating to the Timeline tab. Click **Record** in the bottom control bar, reload the game, and then click the **Events** bar at the top to see a view like Figure 8-3.

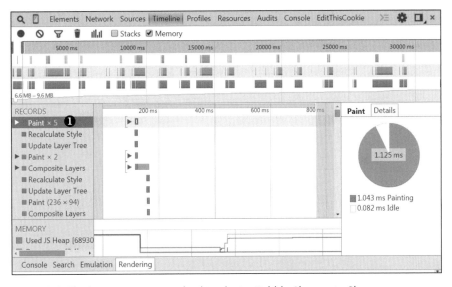

Figure 8-3: The browser events involved in playing Bubble Shooter *in Chrome*

All of the paint events ❶, like those in Figure 8-3, should be highlighted in green on your screen. In the canvas version of the game, a few paint calls occur once a level has been loaded, whereas in the CSS version, such calls occur constantly.

You can use the Timeline tool to identify when paint events happen and minimize them to speed up your game's rendering. Just remember that different browsers may repaint the scene at different times. As always, use the tools available, but also test on your target platforms and devices as the main guide to performance.

In general, minimizing DOM manipulation is the key to minimizing paint operations. Search for articles on minimizing browser reflow and browser paint operations for more detailed and up-to-date information on the inner workings of rendering engines.

Security

If your game has any kind of scoring or progression system, someone will try to cheat it. But the key is to assess the ramifications of having cheats slip through the system and decide whether or not those ramifications are critical. For *Bubble Shooter*, this isn't an issue: if someone wants to set a high score on their local machine, that's up to them. However, for games with an online competitive element or where buying power-ups is a revenue stream, you need to ensure that cheating is difficult to impossible.

We can try to address security in HTML5 games in a few ways.

Trust No One

The simplistic approach to security in any games that run on the client, whether they're built with HTML5, Flash, or even native code, is to not trust anything that the client sends to the server. A POST back to the server with, say, a high score value (as we used in the examples on AJAX and Web-Sockets) is easily forged. The score may be valid, the POST may be forged, or someone may even use a debugging tool to change the high score while the game runs. The server only sees the data as it's received and can't differentiate between a genuine and a cheat POST.

Unfortunately, not trusting the client is often the correct approach: there's no way to completely guarantee the security of code running on the client. The only way to make a game secure is to have all game logic processed by the server. To completely secure *Bubble Shooter*, we'd pass mouse clicks to the server, have the collision and popping logic run on the server, and then pass the results back to the client to animate. This is more difficult to develop and test, and the user would need a constant (and fast) Internet connection to even play the game.

Obfuscation

The server-side approach is essential when a game includes financial transactions, but for many games, obfuscation is good enough. The idea behind obfuscation is to make cheating as difficult as possible, essentially making the effort involved greater than the reward. For example, if a high score is posted to the server as an encoded value, passed with a checksum, and takes hours of reading through code to decipher how it was created, cheaters are unlikely to go through all of that effort just to get to the top of a high score table.

Of course, obfuscation usually comes at the price of readability for you as well as hackers. But there are a number of ways to make code difficult to read, and you can even apply some as a post-build process.

The simplest option is running your code through a *minifier* before you package it for a live environment. Minifiers shorten all long variable names in your code and eliminate whitespace. For example, code such as this:

```
var highScore = 0;
highScore += 20;
```

becomes something like this after minifying:

```
var highScore=0;highScore+=20;
```

Effectively, minifying removes the whitespace and puts everything onto one line. Such minified code quickly becomes difficult to read. You can easily un-minify the line breaks. Many minifiers will also rename variables inside functions. For example, this function:

```
var highScore = (function(){
  var highScore = 0;
  highScore += 20;
  return highScore;
});
```

could become much smaller:

```
var highScore=function(){var a=0;return a+=20};
```

The property that you've been calling `highScore` in your code becomes much harder to find if it's now called a instead!

NOTE *Minifying code also has the added advantage of creating smaller code that should therefore load faster, which is an important consideration when deploying in a web environment. In fact, you should consider minifying your JavaScript code in all web applications.*

Google released a tool called the Closure Compiler, which acts as a minifier along with providing a number of other benefits. It attempts to optimize code, even rewriting it in places, and outputs smaller and sometimes even faster code than the original version. The compiler generates JavaScript, analyzes your code, and raises errors. Declaring variables, keeping track of scope, and maintaining other good practices pay off when you use a minifier such as the Closure Compiler, because the compiler provides greater benefits the clearer and simpler your coding structure is.

You can use the Closure Compiler online or download and run the Java application from *https://developers.google.com/closure/compiler/*. Once you have access to it, paste the Closure Compiler in the JavaScript code that you want to compile and then copy the output. It's recommended that you keep a copy of your original code, because the compiler output is far too difficult to work with if you need to make further changes.

Using Private Variables

Along with post-build processes, you can also code in ways that make it harder for cheaters to follow through code and change it on the fly. For example, private variables make manipulating internal values on the console more difficult. The following has a private variable for highScore:

```
var Game = function(){
  var highScore = 0;
  var getHighScore = function(){ return highScore;};
  return this;
};
```

The variable is considered private because it only exists inside the scope of a Game object. We could have made the variable public as follows:

```
var Game = function(){
  this.highScore = 0;
  var getHighScore = function(){ return this.highScore;};
  return this;
};
```

This would allow the value of highScore to be changed on a Game object just by changing the value of its highScore property. However, in the private version, there's no way to access the value of highScore from outside the object.

If highScore is private, cheaters will have difficulty changing its value without using a program like Firebug to add a breakpoint within the object. They'll have even more trouble if the code is minified and obfuscated. highScore is actually labeled "a", and it's difficult to even find where the high score is updated in the first place.

With a couple of relatively simple steps (making some variables private and minifying our code), we've already narrowed down the potential cheaters from those who know a small amount of JavaScript to those who know it quite well and are willing to take the time to reverse engineer our code. Now, let's look at one more way to prevent cheating.

Validating with Checksums

You can also secure information passed to the server by using checksums to validate the variable passed. The simplest techniques just encode a value so there is at least some check that the number is correct. This won't eliminate cheating, and checksums don't need to be very complicated, but it will ensure that anyone who wants to cheat needs to read and understand your JavaScript code first. For example, if we passed highScore to the server, we could POST something like this:

```
{
  highScore : 9825,
  check : 21
}
```

The value 21 is 9,825 modulus 129 (or highScore%129 in code), where 129 is a number I chose as being big enough to create a range of check values but also being a factor smaller than likely high scores. This almost trivial check actually increases the level of security because now the barrier to posting a fake high score is not only knowing how to POST but also being able to follow through the code to the point where the check value is created. A seasoned JavaScript programmer might find those steps simple, but the average meddling game player probably won't.

The preceding example may be too trivial for your liking, and you can use any process you like for generating a checksum. Common approaches include using hash functions such as MD5, SHA, or CRC32, although the disadvantage of these is that programmers will often recognize the structure well enough to know they are looking at a standard hashing function.

In principle, any process you create that can generate a range of check values will significantly slow down, and possibly discourage, a large number of potential cheaters.

Of course, you may still get a few cheaters whatever you do, because some hackers enjoy the challenge of beating the programmer more than the challenge of beating the game. You can obfuscate as much as you like, and you may end up with code that's almost impossible to read. But remember that you can never guarantee security in client-side code and never fully trust the information passed from the client to the server.

Summary

As you may have gathered from this chapter, browser support for HTML5 is an ever-changing landscape. The good news is that browsers are generally converging on the same standard rather than adding their own features. Also, support for HTML5 is improving all the time.

With the rate of change, it's important to keep up-to-date on which browser features are ready for mainstream usage as well as what's on the horizon. Whether in terms of improved performance, memory management, sound, or 3D features, the capabilities of HTML5 games are constantly advancing.

Further Practice

1. Add fullscreen capability to *Bubble Shooter* in a desktop browser. To make the switch as easy as possible, add a button to the top bar that is visible only if fullscreen mode is supported. Also, change the CSS so that when the page is displayed fullscreen, the game is centered.

2. Write a routine to post the player's score to a fictional server address using jQuery's ajax method. Post the score at the end of each level and write a checksum function to add basic security using your method of choice.

3. Find and test some online minifier and obfuscation services. Compare the file size of the output code to the size of the original source.

AFTERWORD

 Hopefully, working through this book has taught you how simple it can be to develop a game with HTML5 and JavaScript and has given you some insight into these technologies' potential. The next question is: where to next? The answer is: go and make more games!

With your new skills and HTML5, CSS, and JavaScript reference material on the Internet, you should be able to tackle just about any kind of game that's possible with HTML5, although I recommend making your next project relatively small and achievable. Most developers have a list of unfinished projects longer than their list of finished ones, so start with a game that will let you put a tick in the right column.

If you already have some game ideas and think you can build them, by all means dive straight in! In case you're wondering where to go, here are a few suggestions to help you hone your skills and build a portfolio.

Improving Bubble Shooter

Bubble Shooter is pretty nifty already, but we all know it could be better. Any game always has room for improvement! Here are some ideas:

- Add power-ups and bonus points that drop when bubbles are popped and that the user has to click to collect.
- Add more bubble colors to later levels.
- Create grid patterns in different sizes and layouts.
- Implement side walls so the player can bounce fired bubbles off the sides.

You shouldn't need to write an entirely new game to add these features, and with the bulk of *Bubble Shooter* in place already, you can really focus on refining them. Throw in a few creative ideas of your own, and you'll have a game that people can't stop playing!

Creating a Whole New Game

You can learn a lot by spending time polishing a game such as *Bubble Shooter*, but to build your confidence as a game developer, there's nothing better than building as many games as you can. You can either create your own new game ideas or, to fast-track to the programming process, work with some existing games and try to figure out how they're made. I'll describe a few suggestions for basic game ideas that you'll be able to construct with your new skills.

Match-3

Match-3 games, such as *Bejeweled* and *Candy Crush*, never seem to go out of fashion, and they present both a well-defined technical challenge and a demanding user interface one. Consider the problem of a set of gems exploding and dropping, which in turn causes more gems to drop and explode, and so on. Visualize algorithms to handle the cascading effects and consider what happens if the user tries to swap a gem while all of this is happening. Will you let players do that? Try building the best game of this type that you can, and then, once you have it working, play *Bejeweled* or one of the other popular implementations, identify the features you think make the experience fun, and try to add similar polish to your game. Subtle but effective touches really make all the difference.

Solitaire

Card games are simpler than other games graphically, but they pose enough user interface and game logic challenges that it's worth working through one. Once the game logic is in place, you can offer users customized deck backs and animations to give your game personality. Be sure to obfuscate your code so that players can't peek at the deck state while playing!

A Platform Game

A platform game is a big step up from the types of games mentioned earlier. You'll need to implement some basic physics for the main character (although I wouldn't try to implement real physics for the entire game) and some kind of scrolling, either just sideways or possibly in both dimensions. The level design can remain simple: define an entrance point and an exit point and make the player cross between the two. By the end, you'll start thinking more in terms of reusing code for future games, and you'll have solved challenges such as animating a moving figure.

A Simple Physics Game

Angry Birds was a huge hit, which makes it all the more surprising that the basic mechanics are so simple to re-create. *Angry Birds* uses a physics engine called Box2D, and there's a free version available for JavaScript called Box2dWeb. You can find the code and documentation at *https://code.google.com/p/box2dweb/*. The examples that you'll find online aren't always simple to follow, and adding physics to a game is challenging. I recommend Seth Ladd's tutorial for a step-by-step introduction to the library at *http://blog.sethladd.com/2011/08/box2d-orientation-for-javascript.html*.

Joining a Game Development Team

If none of the ideas discussed so far captures your imagination, and you're struggling to come up with a game concept of your own, consider finding a game designer who's looking for someone to help realize their creations. Sites such as Meetup (*http://meetup.com/*) are a good place to look for game development groups. You can meet and perhaps collaborate with both established and aspiring game developers.

With HTML5, an individual or a small team can create games that mass audiences can play on desktop and mobile devices more easily than ever before. Grab the opportunity—go forth and make games!

INDEX

The Electronic Frontier Foundation (EFF) is the leading organization defending civil liberties in the digital world. We defend free speech on the Internet, fight illegal surveillance, promote the rights of innovators to develop new digital technologies, and work to ensure that the rights and freedoms we enjoy are enhanced — rather than eroded — as our use of technology grows.

EFF.ORG

ELECTRONIC FRONTIER FOUNDATION

Protecting Rights and Promoting Freedom on the Electronic Frontier

Build an HTML5 Game is set in New Baskerville, Futura, Dogma, and TheSansMono Condensed. The book was printed and bound by Lake Book Manufacturing in Melrose Park, Illinois. The paper is 60# Husky Opaque Offset Smooth, which is certified by the Sustainable Forestry Initiative (SFI).

The book uses a layflat binding, in which the pages are bound together with a cold-set, flexible glue, and the first and last pages of the resulting book block are attached to the cover. The cover is not actually glued to the book's spine, and when open, the book lies flat and the spine doesn't crack.

UPDATES

Visit *http://nostarch.com/html5game/* for updates, errata, and other information.

More no-nonsense books from  **NO STARCH PRESS**

ELOQUENT JAVASCRIPT, 2ND EDITION
A Modern Introduction to Programming
by MARIJN HAVERBEKE
DECEMBER 2014, 472 PP., $39.95
ISBN 978-1-59327-584-6

JAVASCRIPT FOR KIDS
A Playful Introduction to Programming
by NICK MORGAN
DECEMBER 2014, 336 PP., $34.95
ISBN 978-1-59327-408-5
full color

IF HEMINGWAY WROTE JAVASCRIPT
by ANGUS CROLL
OCTOBER 2014, 192 PP., $19.95
ISBN 978-1-59327-585-3

THE BOOK OF CSS3
A Developer's Guide to the Future of Web Design
by PETER GASSTON
NOVEMBER 2014, 304 PP., $34.95
ISBN 978-1-59327-580-8

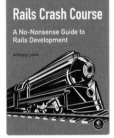

RAILS CRASH COURSE
A No-Nonsense Guide to Rails Development
by ANTHONY LEWIS
OCTOBER 2014, 296 PP., $34.95
ISBN 978-1-59327-572-3

BUILD YOUR OWN WEBSITE
A Comic Guide to HTML, CSS, and WordPress
by NATE COOPER, *with art by* KIM GEE
SEPTEMBER 2014, 264 PP., $19.95
ISBN 978-1-59327-522-8

PHONE:
800.420.7240 OR
415.863.9900

EMAIL:
SALES@NOSTARCH.COM

WEB:
WWW.NOSTARCH.COM